Sunset

Low-Fat Mexican

COOK BOOK

By the Editors of Sunset Books and Sunset Magazine

Sunset Publishing Corporation ■ Menlo Park, California

A glossy golden pepper makes an edible bowl for colorful, nutritious Red & Yellow Pepper Salad-Salsa (recipe on page 44).

Research & Text
Karyn I. Lipman

Special Consultant
Patricia Kearney, R.D.
Clinical Dietitian
Stanford University Hospital
Stanford, California

Coordinating Editor
Linda J. Selden

Design
Joe di Chiarro

Illustrations
Guy Porfirio

Photography
Peter Christiansen: 2; **Norman A. Plate:** 74; **Nikolay Zurek:** 7, 10, 15, 18, 23, 26, 31, 34, 39, 42, 47, 50, 55, 58, 63, 66, 71, 79, 82, 87, 90, 95, 98, 103, 106, 111, 114, 119, 122, 127.

Photo Styling
Susan Massey

Fresh Ways with Mexican Flavors

Do you love the zest and fresh, great flavors of Mexican cooking? Are enchiladas, tacos, and vibrant salsas among your favorite foods? And are you interested in trimming fat from your meals? If you answered "yes" to any of these questions, this book is for you. Throughout these pages, you'll find dozens of lean, delicious Mexican-style recipes. From classics like Fiesta Enchiladas to fresh, bright vegetable dishes such as Seasoned Sweet Corn to a whole chapter of tempting desserts, our selections prove that you can make great Mexican meals without loading up on fat or sacrificing great taste.

In addition to eight chapters of recipes, we've included two pages of menu ideas. At the end of the book, you'll find an appendix giving information on typical Mexican ingredients, with a focus on fresh and dried chiles.

All our recipes have been developed to conform to the American Heart Association recommendations for fat intake; in each, fat provides less than 30% of the calories.

For our recipes, we provide a nutritional analysis (see page 6) prepared by Hill Nutrition Associates, Inc., of Florida. We thank Lynne Hill, R.D., for her advice and expertise.

We are grateful to Dr. Paul W. Bosland, Associate Professor of Horticulture at New Mexico State University, for his thorough review of our information on chiles. We also thank Rebecca LaBrum for editing the manuscript. Our thanks to Beaver Brothers Antiques, Fillamento, Forrest Jones, and RH for accessories used in our photographs.

All of the recipes in this book were tested and developed in the Sunset test kitchens.

Senior Editor (Food and Entertaining), Sunset Magazine
Jerry Anne Di Vecchio

Cover: Colorful, appealing Black Bean & Fresh Corn Nachos (recipe on page 12) are superb as an appetizer or a main course. Top the combination of black beans, sweet corn, and jalapeño jack cheese with tart Lime Salsa (recipe on page 33), then scoop up each bite with water-crisped corn tortilla chips (recipe on page 25). The crunchy chips are great with Creamy Guacamole (page 29), too. Design by Susan Bryant. Photography by Nikolay Zurek. Photo styling by Liz Ross. Food styling by Karyn I. Lipman.

Editor, Sunset Books: Elizabeth L. Hogan

First printing January 1994

CONTENTS

Special Features

LOWFAT

MEXICAN

COOKING

If you love the vibrant flavors of Mexico but worry that your favorite dishes just don't suit a lowfat diet, think again. The pages of this book are filled with lean, delicious Mexican recipes; some are well-known classics, others nontraditional choices inspired by ingredients commonly used in Mexican cuisine. Perhaps the very best news is that you can enjoy all these wonderful dishes with only minimal changes in your cooking style. As you'll see, our recipes simply take advantage of the naturally healthful foods that Mexican cooks have always favored: fresh fruits and vegetables, hearty legumes and whole grains, and lean meats, poultry, and fish.

Bringing Mexico to Your Kitchen

Among the world's great cuisines, the cooking of Mexico stands out for its color, creativity, and complexity of flavor and texture. And as this book will show you, Mexican cuisine can be just as lean and healthful as it is flavorful. To develop the satisfying lightened-up dishes in these pages, we've followed just a few simple guidelines. As a rule, we keep the addition of fat to a minimum and emphasize fresh, nutrient-dense ingredients. Many of the foods we use—beans, corn, raw vegetables and fruits—are naturally rich in fiber. Whenever possible, low- or reduced-sodium products are used in place of their high-sodium "regular" counterparts. And the focus is always on lean cooking methods: baking, grilling, broiling, steaming, and stove-top braising with very little fat.

The Mexican-style favorites you'll enjoy include Fiesta Enchiladas (page 19), Chili Verde (page 54), crab-topped soft tacos (page 14), and, of course, nachos (pages 12 and 13) and refried beans (page 57). For streamlined *sopaipillas* (page 102), we've used a traditional dough—but instead of deep-frying the breads, we first boil them, then bake them chewy-crisp. And how about a shortcut version of the famous *mole poblano*? Our lowfat Jalapeño Chicken with Mole Poblano (page 59) is just as irresistible as the original, but it's much easier to prepare.

If you have a sweet tooth, you'll be delighted with our desserts. Many are based on fresh fruits; you'll find chimichangas filled with juicy cherries (page 116), a strawberry-kiwi "salsa" to enjoy with cinnamon tortilla chips (page 116), and refreshing, jewel-bright soups (page 108). Other choices, such as luscious Double Caramel Flan (page 109) and creamy Raisin Rice Pudding (page 115), get a nutritional boost from eggs and plenty of nonfat milk. We've included cakes, too. When you're in the mood for something special, try a slice of Mexican Cocoa Cake (page 110)—fragrant with cinnamon and almonds, deliciously moist, and incredibly low in fat.

As you look through the following chapters, you'll also discover hard-to-come-by recipes for regional foods. *Semitas* (page 100) have been enjoyed in Puebla for years; now you too can share these crusty, top-hatted rolls with family and friends. Or enjoy Birria-style Brisket (page 57), a tempting stew from the mountains of Zacatecas in central Mexico. Seasoned with mild chiles, spices, vinegar, and plenty of onions, this slow-cooked beef roast makes a marvelous filling for enchiladas, tacos, or burritos.

Throughout the book are single-subject features focusing on Mexican specialties. Tortillas, of course, are basic to Mexican meals, and on page 25 we offer several ways to present them: warmed to use for burritos or soft tacos, baked whole for crisp taco shells, or cut into wedges or strips and baked to an appetizing crunch for lowfat chips and garnishes. Salsas, too, are a standard on Mexican tables. We offer a rainbow of choices on pages 32 and 33, from a bright cherry tomato version to sweeter combinations based on pineapple and papaya. Page 49 presents a pair of seviches—tart seafood salads to enjoy as a first course or a light entrée. And on pages 112 and 113, you'll find a collection of favorite Mexican-style drinks, including cold punches, margaritas, and hot, cinnamon-scented coffee.

Shopping for Mexican Ingredients

For a quick review of the fundamental elements of Mexican cuisine, turn to the appendix beginning on page 118. You'll doubtless be familiar with many of the foods featured; basics like chiles, cilantro, pine nuts, and jicama have long since become standard ingredients in our everyday cooking.

But other foods—achiote and piloncillo, for example—may be new to you. Still, even for these, you probably won't have to hunt much farther than a well-stocked grocery store or specialty-foods store. It's a good idea, though, to seek out a nearby Mexican market for some of the more unusual ingredients. Such stores also offer fresh and dried chiles and other basic foods and seasonings in greater variety than you'll typically find in most supermarkets.

Using Our Recipes

It's easy to put together lowfat Mexican meals. To spark your interest and enthusiasm, take a look at the menus on pages 8 and 9; you'll find suggestions for combining a variety of our recipes to make lean, flavor-rich Mexican-style breakfasts, lunches, and dinners.

Accompanying every recipe are cooking and preparation times and a detailed nutritional analysis. The introduction to each recipe offers other useful information. Besides learning how a dish looks or tastes, you may discover a bit about its origin, how we've lightened it up, or where to find its key ingredients. Or we might mention how a dish is traditionally served or give tips for presenting it at home.

While no special equipment is needed for the recipes in this book, there are a few common Mexican cooking utensils that should be used with caution. Keep in mind that low-fire glazed pottery, including earthenware pots (*ollas*) and casseroles (*cazuellas*), can leach unacceptable amounts of lead into foods if the foods placed in it are acidic or liquid. To be on the safe side, use this

kind of pottery only for serving dry foods such as breads, tortillas, or whole fruits. If you're concerned about a particular piece of pottery, test it for leachable lead, using one of the inexpensive test kits sold at hardware stores.

A Word About Our Nutritional Data

For our recipes, we provide a nutritional analysis stating calorie count; percentage of calories from fat; grams of protein, carbohydrates, total fat, and saturated fat; and milligrams of cholesterol and sodium. Generally, the analysis applies to a single serving, based on the number of servings given for each recipe and the amount of each ingredient. If a range is given for the number of servings and/or the amount of an ingredient, the analysis is based on an average of the figures given.

The nutritional analysis does not include optional ingredients or those for which no specific amount is stated. If an ingredient is listed with a substitution, the information was calculated using the first choice.

*A bowl of silky-smooth Golden Pepper Bisque (recipe on page 40) and a
glass of chilled white wine add up to a superbly simple lunch. Dress up each
serving of the mellow pepper-potato purée with crisp Garlic Croutons
(recipe on page 48), shredded cheese, and a little olive oil.*

Lowfat Mexican Menus

Wouldn't it be festive to dine in Mexico today? Whatever you're longing for—a sunny patio brunch, a formal dinner, a barbecue fiesta—you'll find inspiration on these pages. The menus below range from traditional to more innovative; just choose the meal that suits your mood. Adjust the recipe choices and the numbers of servings to fit your crowd—then serve up a Mexican feast.

South-of-the-Border Breakfast

For a healthy approach to breakfast, serve eggs poached in a light tomato-chile sauce, with a big basket of warm tortillas alongside. Rich but lean Mexican Hot Cocoa and your choice of fresh fruit complete this lowfat meal for four.

Drowned Eggs (page 85)
Warm Corn Tortillas (page 25)
Sliced Bananas, Oranges, or Pineapple Spears
Mexican Hot Cocoa (page 113)

Bountiful Brunch

This simple, filling menu for six is designed with make-ahead preparation in mind. A day in advance, bake the bread and nachos and start the soufflé batter; before your guests arrive, simply complete the soufflés. Be sure everyone is seated at the table when the soufflés come out of the oven, since they'll fall upon cooling.

Spiced Bell Pepper Soufflés (page 88)
Cucumber & Green Onion Salad (page 45)
Easy Corn-Cheese Bread (page 94)
Dessert Nachos (page 116)
Mexican Coffee (page 112)
Fresh Orange Juice

A Sampler of Mexican Favorites

Gather family and friends for a warming, casual buffet of all-time favorites. To maintain the traditional Mexican theme, serve the meal at midday—and follow it with a relaxing siesta! The menu serves six to eight (if you choose Spirited Margaritas, you'll need to double the recipe).

Corn Salsa (page 33)
Water-crisped Tortilla Chips (page 25)
Fiesta Enchiladas (page 19)
Soft Crab Tacos (page 14)
Chiles Rellenos Casserole (page 84)
Zesty Refried Beans (page 57)
Mexican Rice (page 81)
Double Caramel Flan (page 109)
Spirited or Nonalcoholic Margaritas (page 113)

Picnic with Panache

Here's a delicious way to enjoy an outdoor meal at a relaxed pace. Just set out a variety of cold dishes, keeping the emphasis on finger foods; only the soup and salad require utensils. There's plenty here to serve six to eight, though you will have to make a double batch of lemonade.

Turkey Jerky (page 30)
Golden Tomato-Papaya Gazpacho (page 38)
Roasted Pepper & Black Bean Salad (page 76)
Cornbread (page 92)
Fresh Mangoes & Papayas
Cocoa Pepper Cookies (page 97)
Chile-Mint Lemonade (page 112) or Assorted Fruit Juices

Light & Lively All-vegetable Buffet

This delightfully easy springtime menu for four unites a selection of five colorful, refreshing dishes. All take advantage of the season's best produce, and all can be made ahead. For a festive drink, dress up plain mineral water with one of the exotic fruit nectars or juices sold in Mexican markets.

Chilled Cucumber & Cilantro Soup (page 37)

Red Pepper Flan (page 88)

Black Bean & Jicama Salad (page 76)

Double Corn Biscuits (page 94)

Oranges with Rum Syrup & Spiced Cream (page 117)

Sparkling Mineral Water

Fruit Nectar or Juice

Easygoing Barbecue

On a lazy summer afternoon or evening, serve up a menu that's perfect for outdoor dining. The potato-carrot salad, corn, and cake can be made in advance, and they keep well without refrigeration. The meal serves six.

Seasoned Sweet Corn (page 73)

Roasted Potatoes & Carrots with Citrus Dressing (page 69)

Carne Asada (page 52)

Warm Tortillas (page 25)

Mexican Cocoa Cake (page 110)

Beer or Soft Drinks

North-of-the-Border Fiesta

Though inspired by Mexican flavors, the choices in this menu originated north of the border. To serve 8 to 10, you'll need to double the fajita, chimichanga, and iced tea recipes.

Black Bean & Fresh Corn Nachos (page 12)

Bulgur Relish (page 80)

Oven-baked Turkey Fajitas (page 17)

Cherry Chimichangas (page 116)

Hibiscus Iced Tea (page 112)

Winter Soup Special

On a cold night, nothing is as comforting as a bowl of hearty soup served with thick slices of warm, home-baked bread. To conclude this dinner for six, offer a homey dessert, too: a spicy bread pudding served with smooth pumpkin custard.

Caesar Salad (page 48)

Turkey Albondigas Soup (page 36)

Graham & Cornmeal Yeast Bread (page 99)

Cinnamon Bread Pudding with Pumpkin Custard (page 115)

Coffee or Hot Tea

Elegant Mexican Menu

Mexico's deservedly famous *mole poblano* is a popular item on the menus of fine restaurants—and a great choice for an elegant at-home meal. The sophisticated menu below is sure to delight a group of eight special guests (you'll want to double the coffee recipe).

Picadillo-stuffed Empanadas (page 28)

Orange-Onion Salad with Red Chile Dressing (page 46)

Jalapeño Chicken with Mole Poblano (page 59)

Hot Rice

Warm Corn Tortillas (page 25)

Drunken Cake (page 110)

Mexican Coffee (page 112) or Milk

A Seafood Sampler

Succulent seafood is the star in this light but satisfying dinner for six. Make the seviche and soup ahead of time, then chill until ready to serve. You'll need to double or triple the tilapia recipe.

Lime & Chipotle Scallop Seviche (page 49)

Sliced Tomatoes & Cucumbers

Whole Tilapia with Onion & Lemon (page 64)

Green Rice with Pistachios (page 80)

Cactus Pear & Tree Pear Soup (page 108)

Chilled White Wine or Sparkling Mineral Water

Top smoky refried black beans with sweet corn and jalapeño jack cheese to
make these Black Bean & Fresh Corn Nachos (recipe on page 12). Serve with
Lime Salsa (recipe on page 33), homemade corn tortilla chips (recipe on
page 25), and a pitcher of Hibiscus Iced Tea (recipe on page 112).

A L L - T I M E

F A V O R I T E S

Whether you're entertaining friends or treating the family, tempt diners with Mexican-style classics, from hearty enchiladas and tostadas to enticing soft tacos and sizzling fajitas. This chapter is brimming with long-time favorites, all as rich in flavor as they're high in good nutrition and low in fat.

Pictured on page 10

Black Bean & Fresh Corn Nachos

Preparation time: About 20 minutes

Cooking time: About 25 minutes

Though created north of the border, this colorful entrée or appetizer was inspired by three Mexican staples: black beans, corn, and tortillas.

> About 1½ cups Lime Salsa (page 33)
> **Refried Black Beans (page 57)**
> 4 **cups cooked yellow or white corn kernels (from 4 large ears corn); or 2 packages (about 10 oz. *each*) frozen corn kernels, thawed**
> 1 **cup (about 4 oz.) shredded jalapeño jack cheese**
> **About 12 cups water-crisped corn tortilla chips (page 25) or purchased tortilla chips**
> **Cilantro leaves**

1. Prepare Lime Salsa and refrigerate.

2. Prepare Refried Black Beans. Spoon beans onto a large, ovenproof rimmed platter; spread out evenly to make an oval. Top beans evenly with corn, then sprinkle with cheese. Bake in a 400° oven until hot in center (about 10 minutes).

3. Remove bean mixture from oven. Tuck some of the tortilla chips around edge of platter; serve remaining chips alongside. Garnish with cilantro.

4. To serve, spoon bean mixture onto plates; top with some of the Lime Salsa. To eat, scoop bean mixture onto chips; add more salsa to taste. Makes 8 main-dish or 12 appetizer servings.

Per main-dish serving: 423 calories (24% calories from fat), 18 g protein, 67 g carbohydrates, 12 g total fat (4 g saturated fat), 22 mg cholesterol, 668 mg sodium

Carnitas Nachos

Preparation time: About 15 minutes

Cooking time: 2 to 2¼ hours

Tender turkey, shredded or torn into chunks, is appropriately called *carnitas*—"little meats." Here, it's served with beans and chips for a satisfying main dish or starter.

> **About 1½ cups Watermelon Pico de Gallo (page 33)**
> 1½ **pounds skinless, boneless turkey thighs, cut into 1½-inch pieces**
> 1 **can (about 14½ oz.) low-sodium chicken broth**
> 1 **clove garlic, minced or pressed**
> 1 **dry bay leaf**
> ½ **teaspoon dry oregano**
> ¼ **cup canned diced green chiles**
> 2 **tablespoons distilled white vinegar**
> **Refried Cannellini Beans (recipe follows)**
> 1 **cup (about 4 oz.) shredded jack cheese**
> **About 8 cups water-crisped flour tortilla chips (page 25) or purchased tortilla chips**

1. Prepare Watermelon Pico de Gallo and refrigerate.

2. Place turkey in a 2- to 3-quart pan. Cover and cook over medium heat to draw out juices (8 to 10 minutes). Uncover, increase heat to high, and cook, stirring often, until liquid has evaporated and meat is well browned (10 to 12 minutes).

3. Add broth, garlic, bay leaf, and oregano; stir to scrape browned bits free. Bring to a boil; then reduce heat, cover, and simmer until turkey is very tender when pierced (about 1 hour). Uncover; bring to a boil over high heat, then boil until all liquid has evaporated (5 to 10 minutes). Add chiles and vinegar; stir to scrape browned bits free. Remove from heat. Shred turkey, using 2 forks (or let turkey cool, then pull it apart with your fingers).

4. Prepare Refried Cannellini Beans. Spoon beans onto a large, ovenproof rimmed platter; spread out evenly to make a 10-inch round. Top evenly with shredded turkey. (At this point, you may let cool, then cover and refrigerate until next day.) Bake, covered, in a 400° oven until hot in center (15 to 25 minutes; about 35 minutes if refrigerated). Uncover and sprinkle with cheese. Continue to bake, uncovered, until cheese is melted (about 5 more minutes).

5. Remove turkey mixture from oven. Tuck some of the tortilla chips around edge of platter; serve remaining chips and Watermelon Pico de Gallo alongside.

6. To eat, scoop turkey mixture onto chips; add pico de gallo to taste. Makes 6 to 8 main-dish or 10 to 12 appetizer servings.

Refried Cannellini Beans. Heat 1 tablespoon **olive oil** in a wide frying pan over medium-high heat. Add 1 large **onion,** chopped; cook, stirring often, until onion begins to brown (8 to 10 minutes). Add ¾ cup **canned diced green chiles** and 2 cans (about 15 oz. *each*) **cannellini** (white kidney beans), drained and rinsed. Cook, stirring often, using back of spoon or a potato masher to mash beans coarsely, until mixture is slightly thickened (about 5 minutes). Remove from heat.

Per main-dish serving: 420 calories (28% calories from fat), 34 g protein, 42 g carbohydrates, 13 g total fat (2 g saturated fat), 87 mg cholesterol, 519 mg sodium

Pork, Beef & Bean Nachos

Preparation time: About 20 minutes

Cooking time: About 1 hour

Lean pork, beef, and beans combine in these impressive nachos. To complete a savory eat-out-of-hand supper dish or appetizer, offer plenty of crunchy baked tortilla chips.

- 8 **ounces pork tenderloin, trimmed of fat and silvery membrane**
- 8 **ounces beef sirloin steak, trimmed of fat**
- 2 **large onions, chopped**
- 2 **teaspoons chili powder**
- 2 **teaspoons dry oregano**
- ¾ **teaspoon cumin seeds**
- ½ **teaspoon crushed red pepper flakes**
- ¼ **teaspoon ground cinnamon**
- 3 **cups low-sodium chicken broth**
- 6 **tablespoons cider vinegar**
  Salt
- 2 **cans (about 15 oz. *each*) pinto beans, drained and rinsed; or 4 cups cooked (about 2 cups dried) pinto beans, drained and rinsed**
- 1 **small can (about 4 oz.) diced green chiles**
- 1 **cup (about 4 oz.) shredded longhorn cheese**
  Toppings (directions follow)
  About 8 cups water-crisped corn tortilla chips (page 25) or purchased tortilla chips
  Lime wedges

1. Cut pork and beef into chunks and whirl in a food processor just until minced (or grind through medium blade of a food chopper). Set aside.

2. In a wide nonstick frying pan, stir together half the onions, chili powder, 1½ teaspoons of the oregano, ½ teaspoon of the cumin seeds, red pepper flakes, cinnamon, and 1 cup of the broth. Bring to a boil over high heat; boil, stirring often, until liquid has evaporated and browned bits stick to pan. Then add 2 tablespoons water, stirring to scrape browned bits free; cook until mixture begins to brown again.

Repeat this deglazing step, adding 2 tablespoons water each time, until onions are a rich brown color. Add 2 tablespoons more water, then meat; cook, breaking meat up with a spoon, until drippings begin to brown. Repeat deglazing step, adding vinegar in 2-tablespoon portions (and more water, if needed), until mixture is a rich brown color. Season to taste with salt, transfer to a bowl, and set aside.

3. In frying pan, combine remaining onion, ½ teaspoon oregano, and ¼ teaspoon cumin seeds. Stir in 1 cup of the broth. Boil dry, brown, and deglaze as directed above, adding water in 2-tablespoon portions, until mixture is light brown. Add beans and remaining 1 cup broth. Mash beans in pan, then stir over medium-high heat until mixture is thick enough to scoop. Season to taste with salt. (At this point, you may cover and refrigerate meat mixture and beans separately until next day.)

4. Spoon beans onto a large, ovenproof rimmed platter (about 15 inches wide) and spread out evenly. Top beans evenly with meat mixture; sprinkle with chiles, then cheese. Bake, uncovered, in a 400° oven until hot in center (15 to 20 minutes). Remove from oven and add toppings. Tuck some of the tortilla chips around edge of platter; serve remaining chips alongside.

5. To eat, scoop bean mixture onto chips. Serve with lime wedges. Makes 5 main-dish or 8 to 10 appetizer servings.

Toppings. Pit and peel ½ small firm-ripe **avocado;** cut into 6 wedges and moisten with **cider or wine vinegar.** Arrange slices on bean mixture. Sprinkle with ½ cup sliced **green onions,** ¼ cup **cilantro leaves,** and 3 or 4 **pitted large ripe olives.** Mound ¼ cup **plain nonfat yogurt** or reduced-fat sour cream in center; top with a **red or green pickled pepper.**

Per main-dish serving: 540 calories (27% calories from fat), 39 g protein, 62 g carbohydrates, 16 g total fat (7 g saturated fat), 81 mg cholesterol, 833 mg sodium

avajo Tacos

Preparation time: About 10 minutes

Cooking time: 3½ to 4 hours

The traditional "Navajo taco" is a puffy round of fried bread topped with meat and beans. Our lightened-up version of the popular snack uses a flour tortilla as the base; the topping is a lean, spicy mixture of ground turkey and simmered Great Northern beans.

> **Chili Beans (recipe follows)**
> **About 2 cups Cherry Tomato Salsa (page 32) or other salsa of your choice**
> 6 **crisp flour taco shells (page 25)**
> ⅔ **cup shredded Cheddar cheese**
> 4 **cups finely shredded lettuce**
> **Plain nonfat yogurt**

1. Prepare Chili Beans. While beans are simmering, prepare Cherry Tomato Salsa; refrigerate.

2. To assemble tacos, place one taco shell on each of 6 dinner plates. Top equally with cheese, Chili Beans, and lettuce. Spoon ¼ cup salsa and 1 tablespoon yogurt onto each taco; add more salsa and yogurt to taste. Makes 6 servings.

Chili Beans. Sort 1 cup **dried Great Northern or pinto beans,** discarding any debris; rinse beans well. Place beans and 4 cups **water** in a 3- to 4-quart pan; bring to a boil over high heat. Boil, uncovered, for 10 minutes. Remove from heat, cover, and let stand for 1 hour. Drain beans, pour out of pan, and set aside.

Crumble 1 pound **ground turkey breast** into pan; add 1 large **onion,** chopped. Cover tightly and cook over medium heat to draw out juices (15 to 20 minutes); stir occasionally. Uncover and boil over high heat, stirring often, until liquid has evaporated and browned bits stick to pan. Add ¼ cup **water** and stir to scrape browned bits free. Boil, stirring often, until liquid has evaporated and browned bits stick to pan. Add ¼ cup more **water** and boil dry again.

Add 3 cups **low-sodium chicken broth** to pan; stir to scrape browned bits free. Add beans; 1 tablespoon **chili powder;** 2 cloves **garlic,** minced or pressed; and 2 teaspoons *each* **ground cumin,** **dry oregano,** and **dry basil.** Bring to a boil over high heat; then reduce heat, cover, and simmer until beans are tender to bite (1½ to 2 hours). Uncover and boil over high heat, stirring often, until reduced to 4 cups (5 to 7 minutes). Season to taste with **salt.** If made ahead, let cool; then cover and refrigerate for up to 3 days. To reheat, bring to a simmer over medium heat, stirring often.

Per serving: 426 calories (19% calories from fat), 36 g protein, 51 g carbohydrates, 9 g total fat (4 g saturated fat), 61 mg cholesterol, 354 mg sodium

Pictured on facing page

Soft Crab Tacos

Preparation time: About 10 minutes

Cooking time: About 20 minutes

For a quick weekday lunch or supper, try soft tacos topped with shredded lettuce and a blend of chiles, fresh tomatoes, and delicate crabmeat.

> **About 1½ cups Pineapple Salsa (page 33)**
> 2 **tablespoons olive oil**
> 1 **clove garlic, minced or pressed**
> 1 **small red onion, finely chopped**
> 1 **small can (about 4 oz.) diced green chiles**
> 2 **large firm-ripe tomatoes (about 1 lb.** *total***), chopped**
> 1 **pound cooked crabmeat**
> 3 **cups finely shredded lettuce**
> 6 **to 12 warm corn tortillas (page 25)**
> **Thinly sliced green onions**
> **Salt**

1. Prepare Pineapple Salsa and refrigerate.

2. Heat oil in a wide frying pan over medium-high heat. Add garlic and red onion; cook, stirring often, until onion begins to brown (8 to 10 minutes). Add chiles and half the tomatoes; simmer, stirring occasionally, until tomatoes are soft (8 to 10 minutes). Remove from heat; stir in crab.

3. Divide lettuce equally among tortillas; then top tortillas equally with crab mixture and remaining tomatoes. Add green onions, Pineapple Salsa, and salt to taste. Makes 6 servings.

Per serving: 218 calories (28% calories from fat), 18 g protein, 22 g carbohydrates, 7 g total fat (1 g saturated fat), 76 mg cholesterol, 378 mg sodium

For light, elegant dining, you can't go wrong with Soft Crab Tacos (recipe on facing page). A savory combination of crabmeat, mild chiles, lettuce, and tomatoes is topped with juicy Pineapple Salsa (recipe on page 33) and a cilantro-sprig garnish.

FAJITAS

Along the Mexican border, *fajitas* means a long strip of beef, usually skirt steak. Elsewhere, however, the word refers to make-it-yourself burritos filled with a variety of meats, poultry, shellfish, or vegetables—first marinated, then cooked and served sizzling-hot.

Though meat and seafood fajitas are traditionally barbecued over a mesquite fire, they can also be baked, broiled, or seared in a hot cast-iron skillet.

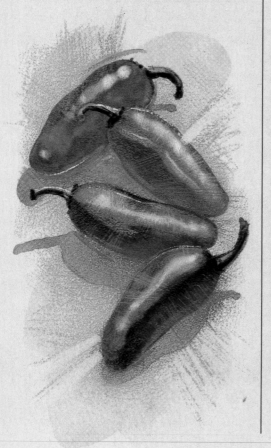

SPICY STEAK FAJITAS

Tender beef strips and onions, infused with the flavors of lime and tequila, cook together quickly for a tempting meal.

1 **pound skirt or flank steak, trimmed of fat**
   Fajita Marinade (recipe follows)
   About 1½ cups Cherry Tomato Salsa (page 32) or other salsa of your choice
   About 1 cup Creamy Guacamole (page 29)
2 **large onions**
   Salad oil
4 **warm flour tortillas (page 25)**
   Plain nonfat yogurt

1. Place steak in a large (1-gallon-size) heavy-duty resealable plastic bag or large nonmetal bowl. Prepare marinade and pour over meat. Seal bag and rotate to coat meat (or turn meat in bowl to coat, then cover airtight). Refrigerate for at least 30 minutes or until next day, turning occasionally.

2. Prepare Cherry Tomato Salsa and Creamy Guacamole; refrigerate.

3. To sauté, lift meat from marinade and drain; discard marinade. Thinly slice meat across the grain, then thinly slice onions; set aside separately. Heat a wide cast-iron or regular frying pan or a shallow oval (about 7- by 9-inch) cast-iron skillet over medium-high heat. When pan is hot enough to make a drop of water bounce, brush it lightly with oil. Add onions to pan and cook, stirring, until soft (about 5 minutes). Increase heat to high. Add meat to pan and cook, stirring, until lightly browned (3 to 4 minutes).

To barbecue, lift meat from marinade and drain; reserve marinade. Cut onions into quarters and brush lightly with oil. Place onions and meat on a lightly greased grill 4 to 6 inches above a solid bed of hot coals. Cook, basting meat and onion several times with reserved marinade and turning as needed to brown evenly, until onions are tinged with brown and meat is done to your liking; cut to test (15 to 20 minutes for rare). Slice onions or pull apart into layers; thinly slice meat across the grain.

To broil, lift meat from marinade and drain; reserve marinade. Place meat on lightly oiled rack of a broiler pan. Thinly slice onions and brush lightly with oil; set alongside meat. Broil meat and onions 3 to 4 inches below heat, basting several times with reserved marinade and turning as needed to brown evenly, until onions are tinged with brown and meat is done to your liking; cut to test (15 to 20 minutes for rare). Thinly slice meat across the grain.

4. To serve, divide meat and onions among tortillas. Add salsa, guacamole, and yogurt to taste. Roll up tortillas to enclose filling; eat out of hand. Makes 4 servings.

Fajita Marinade. In a nonmetal bowl, stir together ½ teaspoon grated **lime peel**; ½ cup **lime juice**; ¼ cup **gold tequila** or nonalcoholic beer; 4 cloves **garlic**, minced or pressed; ½ teaspoon **pepper**; and ½ teaspoon **salt** (optional).

Per serving: 471 calories (29% calories from fat), 36 g protein, 44 g carbohydrates, 15 g total fat (5 g saturated fat), 59 mg cholesterol, 585 mg sodium

BLACK BEAN, CORN & PEPPER FAJITAS

Here's a delicious meatless version of fajitas. Beans, sweet fresh corn, and red bell pepper are marinated in a lively citrus sauce, then warmed and rolled in soft flour tortillas.

¼ cup lime juice
1 tablespoon salad oil
1 teaspoon ground coriander
½ teaspoon ground cumin
2 cans (about 15 oz. *each*) black beans, drained and rinsed; or 4 cups cooked (about 2 cups dried) black beans, drained and rinsed
About 1½ cups cooked yellow or white corn kernels (from 2 medium-size ears corn); or 1 package (about 10 oz.) frozen corn kernels, thawed
1 medium-size red bell pepper (about 6 oz.), seeded and diced
1 fresh jalapeño chile, seeded and minced
About 1½ cups Lime Salsa (page 33) or other salsa of your choice
8 warm flour tortillas (page 25)
½ cup lightly packed chopped cilantro
Salt and pepper

1. In a large (1-gallon-size) heavy-duty resealable plastic bag or large nonmetal bowl, combine lime juice, oil, coriander, and cumin. Seal bag and rotate to mix (or stir well). Add beans, corn, bell pepper, and chile. Seal bag and rotate to coat vegetables (or mix vegetables in bowl, then cover airtight). Refrigerate for at least 20 minutes or until next day.

2. Prepare Lime Salsa; refrigerate.

3. Transfer bean mixture and marinade to a 1½- to 2-quart pan. Heat over medium-high heat just until hot.

4. To eat, scoop out bean mixture with a slotted spoon; drain (discard marinade), then divide among tortillas. Sprinkle evenly with cilantro; add salsa, salt, and pepper to taste. Roll up tortillas to enclose filling; eat out of hand. Makes 8 servings.

Per serving: 335 calories (14% calories from fat), 15 g protein, 59 g carbohydrates, 5 g total fat (1 g saturated fat), 0 mg cholesterol, 177 mg sodium

Pictured on page 18

OVEN-BAKED TURKEY FAJITAS

For a new twist on an old fajita favorite, oven-bake turkey breast with green bell pepper and red onion, then serve the mixture in warm tortillas. Be careful not to overcook the turkey—it's done just as soon as the meat is white in the thickest part.

1 pound turkey breast tenderloins
Lime-Vinegar Marinade (recipe follows)
1 large green bell pepper (about 8 oz.), seeded and cut into eighths
1 large red onion, thinly sliced
About 1 tablespoon salad oil
4 warm flour tortillas (page 25)
Lime wedges

1. Rinse turkey and pat dry. Prepare marinade and pour into a large (1-gallon-size) heavy-duty resealable plastic bag or large nonmetal bowl; add turkey. Seal bag and rotate to coat meat (or turn meat in bowl to coat, then cover airtight). Refrigerate for at least 20 minutes or until next day, turning occasionally.

2. Place bell pepper and onion in a lightly oiled 10- by 15-inch rimmed baking pan. Brush lightly with oil. Bake in a 400° oven for 10 minutes.

Remove from oven. Lift turkey from marinade and arrange alongside pepper and onion, overlapping as little as possible; reserve marinade.

3. Return pan to oven and bake, basting with marinade and turning often, until onion and pepper are tinged with brown and turkey is no longer pink in thickest part; cut to test (about 20 minutes).

4. Thinly slice turkey; then divide turkey, pepper, and onion among tortillas. Roll up tortillas to enclose filling; eat out of hand. Serve with lime wedges. Makes 4 servings.

Lime-Vinegar Marinade. In a nonmetal bowl, stir together ¼ cup **lime juice,** 1 tablespoon **balsamic or red wine vinegar,** 1 clove **garlic** (minced or pressed), ½ teaspoon **honey,** and ¼ teaspoon *each* **ground coriander** and **ground cumin.**

Per serving: 310 calories (20% calories from fat), 32 g protein, 29 g carbohydrates, 7 g total fat (1 g saturated fat), 70 mg cholesterol, 231 mg sodium

18

Fajitas are always a favorite with family and guests—especially when you choose our Oven-baked Turkey Fajitas (recipe on page 17), filled with marinated turkey breast, bell pepper, and red onion. Accompany this eat-out-of-hand specialty with Pickled Vegetables (recipe on page 43) and cold beer.

Fiesta Enchiladas

Preparation time: About 20 minutes

Cooking time: 2¾ to 3 hours

These festive enchiladas are stuffed with pork and served in a flavorful chile sauce. The tortillas are traditionally fried, but we've omitted that step here; we simply soften them in hot water before filling them.

Red Chile Sauce (recipe follows)

1¼ **pounds boneless pork butt or shoulder, trimmed of fat and cut into 1½-inch cubes**

2 **large onions, chopped**

3 **tablespoons chili powder**

2 **teaspoons dry oregano**

3 **cups beef broth**

12 **corn tortillas (6-inch diameter)**

⅓ **cup shredded jack cheese**

1 **large can (about 7 oz.) diced green chiles**

Cilantro sprigs

1. Prepare Red Chile Sauce and set aside.

2. Place pork, onions, and ⅓ cup water in a 5- to 6-quart pan. Cover and cook over medium-high heat for 20 minutes, stirring occasionally. Uncover; cook over high heat, stirring often, until almost all juices have evaporated and browned bits begin to stick to pan (about 20 minutes).

3. Add chili powder, oregano, and broth; stir to scrape browned bits free. Bring mixture to a boil; then reduce heat, cover, and simmer until meat is very tender when pierced (45 minutes to 1 hour). Uncover; cook over high heat, stirring to break meat into shreds, until mixture is reduced to about 3 cups—about 30 minutes. (At this point, you may let cool, then cover and refrigerate until next day.)

4. To assemble enchiladas, immerse a tortilla in a bowl of very hot water until pliable (5 to 15 seconds); drain. Spoon about ¼ cup of the pork filling in center of tortilla; roll to enclose. Set enchilada, seam side down, in a lightly oiled 10- by 15-inch nonstick rimmed baking pan. Repeat to use remaining tortillas, arranging enchiladas in pan in a single layer. Cover pan with foil. (At this point, you may refrigerate for up to 2 hours.)

5. Bake, covered, in a 350° oven until enchiladas are hot in center (about 15 minutes; about 25 min-

utes if refrigerated). Uncover and sprinkle with cheese; continue to bake until cheese is melted (8 to 10 more minutes).

6. Cover a platter with green chiles; top evenly with hot Red Chile Sauce. Set enchiladas in sauce; scatter with cilantro sprigs. Makes 6 servings.

Red Chile Sauce. Lay 8 to 12 **dried red New Mexico or California chiles** (about 3 oz. *total*) in a baking pan. Bake in a 300° oven just until fragrant (3 to 4 minutes). Remove from oven; let cool. Discard stems, seeds, and veins. Rinse and drain chiles; transfer to a 2- to 3-quart pan. Add 2 cups **beef broth,** 2 cloves **garlic** (peeled), ½ teaspoon **dry oregano,** ¼ teaspoon **ground cumin,** and ⅛ teaspoon **ground cloves.** Bring to a boil; then reduce heat, cover, and simmer until chiles are very soft (about 20 minutes).

Whirl chile mixture and 2 teaspoons **cornstarch** in a blender or food processor until smoothly puréed. Pour purée through a fine strainer into a bowl; rub with a spoon to extract liquid. Discard residue. You should have 2 cups; if not, add water to make 2 cups. Return purée to pan; stir over high heat until boiling (or until reduced to 2 cups, if you have over 2 cups chile purée). If made ahead, let cool; then cover and refrigerate for up to 3 days. Reheat before using. Makes about 2 cups.

Per serving: 386 calories (29% calories from fat), 28 g protein, 44 g carbohydrates, 13 g total fat (3 g saturated fat), 67 mg cholesterol, 1,126 mg sodium

Turkey Chorizo Enchiladas

Preparation time: About 15 minutes

Cooking time: About 1½ hours

In these spicy enchiladas, deliciously seasoned turkey sausage provides a flavorful reduced-fat alternative to the traditional pork-based chorizo.

    Red Chile Sauce (page 19)

    Turkey Chorizo Sausage (page 56)

  2 teaspoons cornstarch blended with 1 tablespoon cold water

    Salt (optional)

12 corn tortillas (6-inch diameter)

½ cup shredded Cheddar cheese

¼ cup *each* plain nonfat yogurt and sliced green onions

1. Prepare Red Chile Sauce and set aside.

2. Prepare and cook Turkey Chorizo Sausage as directed. To sausage in frying pan, add ¾ cup of the chile sauce and cornstarch mixture. Bring to a boil over medium heat, stirring; season to taste with salt, if desired.

3. To assemble enchiladas, immerse a tortilla in a bowl of very hot water until pliable (5 to 15 seconds); drain. Spoon a twelfth of the sausage mixture in center of tortilla; roll to enclose. Set enchilada, seam side down, in a 9- by 13-inch baking dish. Repeat to use remaining tortillas, arranging enchiladas in dish in a single layer. (At this point, you may cover and refrigerate for up to 2 hours.)

4. Spoon remaining Red Chile Sauce over enchiladas. Bake, uncovered, in a 350° oven until enchiladas are hot in center (about 15 minutes; about 25 minutes if refrigerated). Sprinkle with cheese and continue to bake until cheese is melted (8 to 10 more minutes). Top with yogurt and onions before serving. Makes 6 servings.

Per serving: 329 calories (21% calories from fat), 28 g protein, 40 g carbohydrates, 8 g total fat (3 g saturated fat), 57 g cholesterol, 639 mg sodium

Chicken-Yogurt Enchilada Casserole

Preparation time: About 15 minutes

Baking time: 45 to 50 minutes

For extra-easy (though nontraditional) enchiladas, cut corn tortillas into strips, layer them with a chicken-yogurt filling, and bake.

  1 cup *each* plain nonfat yogurt and lowfat (1%) cottage cheese

  2 cloves garlic, peeled

  2 teaspoons *each* chili powder, sugar, and cornstarch

  1 tablespoon butter or margarine

¼ cup all-purpose flour

  2 cups low-sodium chicken broth

  1 large can (about 7 oz.) diced green chiles

12 corn tortillas (6-inch diameter)

  2 cups bite-size pieces of cooked chicken

  1 small onion, chopped

½ cup shredded jack cheese

1. In a blender or food processor, whirl yogurt, cottage cheese, garlic, chili powder, sugar, and cornstarch until smoothly puréed. Set aside.

2. Melt butter in a 1½- to 2-quart pan over medium-high heat. Add flour and ⅓ cup water; stir just until bubbly. Whisk in broth; bring to a boil, stirring. Remove from heat; let cool for 5 minutes. Whisk yogurt mixture into flour mixture; stir in chiles. Cover bottom of a 9- by 13-inch baking dish with a third of the yogurt-flour mixture.

3. Dip tortillas, one at a time, in hot water. Drain briefly; cut into 1-inch-wide strips. Scatter half the tortilla strips over yogurt-flour mixture in baking dish; cover with all the chicken and onion, half the jack cheese, and half the remaining yogurt-flour mixture. Top with remaining tortilla strips, yogurt-flour mixture, and jack cheese.

4. Cover dish tightly with foil and bake in a 400° oven for 30 minutes. Uncover; continue to bake until mixture is golden brown on top and appears firm in center when dish is gently shaken (15 to 20 more minutes). Makes 8 servings.

Per serving: 263 calories (26% calories from fat), 20 g protein, 29 g carbohydrates, 8 g total fat (2 g saturated fat), 40 mg cholesterol, 449 mg sodium

Turkey Burritos

Preparation time: 15 minutes

Cooking time: 50 to 60 minutes

Scoop an aromatic turkey filling onto warm tortillas, then embellish with a colorful pepper relish.

       About 1½ cups Spicy Pepper Relish (page 32)
   1   **pound ground turkey or chicken**
   1   **teaspoon salad oil**
   ½   **cup low-sodium chicken broth**
   2   **large onions, chopped**
   2   **cloves garlic, minced or pressed**
   1   **large red bell pepper (about 8 oz.), seeded and chopped**
   1   **can (about 8 oz.) tomato sauce**
   1   **tablespoon lemon juice**
   ½   **teaspoon** *each* **sugar and ground cinnamon**
   ⅛   **teaspoon** *each* **ground cloves, ground nutmeg, and liquid hot pepper seasoning**
   ¼   **cup chopped parsley**
       Salt
   8   **warm flour tortillas (page 25)**
       Plain nonfat yogurt

1. Prepare Spicy Pepper Relish; refrigerate.

2. Crumble turkey into a wide frying pan; add oil. Cook over medium-high heat, stirring often, until meat is crumbly and browned bits stick to pan (about 10 minutes). Add ¼ cup water to pan; stir to scrape browned bits free. Remove pan from heat and transfer turkey to a bowl.

3. To pan, add broth, onions, garlic, and bell pepper. Cook over high heat, stirring occasionally, until pan is almost dry; then stir often until dark brown bits stick to pan. Add 3 to 4 tablespoons water and stir to scrape browned bits free; cook until mixture begins to brown again. Repeat this deglazing step, adding 2 to 3 tablespoons water each time, until mixture is a rich brown color (15 to 20 minutes *total*).

4. Return turkey to pan; add tomato sauce, 1 cup water, lemon juice, sugar, cinnamon, cloves, nutmeg, and hot pepper seasoning. Stir to scrape browned bits free. Bring to a boil over high heat; reduce heat and simmer, uncovered, until reduced to 3 cups (15 to 20 minutes). Stir in parsley; season to taste with salt.

5. To eat, divide turkey filling equally among tortillas. Add yogurt and Spicy Pepper Relish to taste. Roll up tortillas to enclose filling; eat out of hand. Makes 8 servings.

Per serving: 367 calories (19% calories from fat), 15 g protein, 61 g carbohydrates, 8 g total fat (2 g saturated fat), 41 mg cholesterol, 462 mg sodium

All-vegetable Burritos

Preparation time: About 15 minutes

Chilling time: At least 20 minutes

Meatless but surprisingly hearty, these burritos are stuffed with fresh corn, cucumber, and beans.

       Lime Marinade (recipe follows)
   1½ **cups fresh-cut yellow or white corn kernels (from 2 medium-size ears corn); or 1 package (about 10 oz.) frozen corn kernels, thawed**
   1   **can (about 15 oz.) red kidney beans, drained and rinsed; or 2 cups cooked (about 1 cup dried) red kidney beans, drained and rinsed**
   1   **medium-size cucumber (about 8 oz.), peeled, seeded, and finely chopped**
   ½   **cup sliced green onions**
   2   **tablespoons minced cilantro**
   8   **warm flour tortillas (page 25)**

1. Prepare Lime Marinade and pour into a large (1-gallon-size) heavy-duty resealable plastic bag or large nonmetal bowl. Add corn, beans, cucumber, onions, and cilantro. Seal bag; rotate to mix vegetables (or mix vegetables in bowl, then cover airtight). Refrigerate for at least 20 minutes or up to 4 hours; rotate bag (or stir vegetables in bowl) occasionally.

2. To eat, scoop out corn mixture with a slotted spoon; drain (discard marinade), then divide equally among tortillas. Roll up tortillas to enclose filling; eat out of hand. Makes 8 servings.

Lime Marinade. In a nonmetal bowl, stir together 1 teaspoon grated **lime peel;** ⅓ cup **lime juice;** 2 tablespoons **distilled white vinegar;** 1 tablespoon **honey;** 2 teaspoons **Dijon mustard;** 1 teaspoon **ground cumin;** 2 cloves **garlic,** minced or pressed; and 1 **fresh jalapeño chile,** seeded and minced.

Per serving: 189 calories (15% calories from fat), 7 g protein, 34 g carbohydrates, 3 g total fat (0.4 g saturated fat), 0 mg cholesterol, 260 mg sodium

Pictured on facing page

Tamale Pie

Preparation time: About 25 minutes

Baking time: 45 to 55 minutes

Masa biscuits top a rich-tasting, achiote-laced chicken filling in this lean deep-dish version of tamale pie. Purchase the rust-colored achiote condiment in a Mexican market, or mix up a substitute from paprika, herbs, and vinegar (see below).

 3 ounces achiote condiment; or Achiote Substitute (recipe follows)

 2 cups low-sodium chicken broth

 2 tablespoons minced fresh mint or 1 teaspoon dry mint

 ⅛ teaspoon anise seeds

 3 cups bite-size pieces of cooked chicken

 2 large onions, chopped

 2 large tomatoes (about 1 lb. *total*), cut into wedges

 2 tablespoons cornstarch blended with ¼ cup cold water

 Masa Topping (recipe follows)

 Cilantro sprigs (optional)

1. In a 1½- to 2-quart pan, combine achiote condiment (or substitute) with ½ cup of the broth. With a heavy spoon, blend to make a smooth paste. Stir in remaining 1½ cups broth, mint, and anise seeds. Bring to a boil; then reduce heat and simmer for 5 minutes, stirring often to prevent sticking.

2. Mix achiote sauce, chicken, onions, tomatoes, and cornstarch mixture. Spoon into a deep 2- to 3-quart baking dish and spread to make an even layer.

3. Prepare Masa Topping; spoon topping in dollops over filling.

4. Bake on bottom rack of a 400° oven until filling is bubbly in center and topping is well browned (45 to 55 minutes). Let stand for 5 minutes before serving. Garnish with cilantro sprigs, if desired. Makes 6 servings.

Achiote Substitute. In a small bowl, mix 3 tablespoons **paprika,** 2 tablespoons **distilled white vinegar,** 1½ teaspoons **dry oregano,** 3 cloves **garlic** (minced), and ½ teaspoon **ground cumin.**

Masa Topping. In a bowl, combine ½ cup **masa harina** (dehydrated masa flour), ½ cup **all-purpose flour,** and 1½ teaspoons **baking powder.** Add 1 large **egg white,** 1½ tablespoons **salad oil,** and ½ cup **nonfat milk;** stir just until blended.

Per serving: 332 calories (28% calories from fat), 27 g protein, 34 g carbohydrates, 10 g total fat (2 g saturated fat), 63 mg cholesterol, 231 mg sodium

Chicken Chimichangas

Preparation time: About 15 minutes

Cooking time: About 40 minutes

These oven-baked chimichangas offer all the authentic flavor of their traditional deep-fried counterparts, but they're lower in fat.

 Shredded Chicken Filling (page 56)

 About 1½ cups Cucumber & Jicama Salsa (page 32) or other salsa of your choice

 5 cups shredded lettuce

 1½ cups shredded carrots

 8 flour tortillas (7- to 9-inch diameter)

 About ⅓ cup nonfat milk

 ½ cup shredded Cheddar cheese

 Plain nonfat yogurt

1. Prepare Shredded Chicken Filling; set aside. Prepare Cucumber & Jicama Salsa; refrigerate. In a small bowl, mix lettuce and carrots; set aside.

2. To assemble each chimichanga, brush both sides of a tortilla liberally with milk; let stand briefly to soften tortilla. Spoon an eighth of the filling down center of tortilla; top with 1 tablespoon of the cheese. Lap ends of tortilla over filling; then fold sides to center to make a packet. Place chimichanga, seam side down, on a lightly oiled 12- by 15-inch baking sheet and brush with milk. Repeat to make 7 more chimichangas.

3. Bake in a 500° oven, brushing with milk after 5 minutes, until golden brown (8 to 10 minutes).

4. To serve, divide lettuce mixture among 8 plates; place one chimichanga on each plate. Add salsa and yogurt to taste. Makes 8 servings.

Per serving: 291 calories (26% calories from fat), 19 g protein, 37 g carbohydrates, 9 g total fat (3 g saturated fat), 38 mg cholesterol, 338 mg sodium

*Like classic cornhusk-wrapped tamales, Tamale Pie (recipe on facing page)
has a succulent meat filling and a masa "crust"—but it's quickly and easily
assembled in a casserole dish. Our lean version of this savory entrée features
a chicken-tomato filling flavored with achiote, mint, and anise.*

Shredded Beef Tostadas

Preparation time: About 20 minutes

Cooking time: About 1¼ hours

Smoky chipotle chiles and plenty of garlic and spices give this slow-cooked mixture of beef and turkey sausage its rich, complex flavor. Spoon the filling over shredded lettuce on crisp corn tortillas for a great tostada meal.

> 3 cups Tinga (recipe follows), Shredded Chicken Filling (page 56), or other shredded meat filling of your choice
>
> About 1½ cups Corn Salsa (page 33) or other salsa of your choice
>
> 6 crisp corn taco shells (page 25) or warm corn tortillas (page 25)
>
> 2 cups shredded lettuce
>
> Plain nonfat yogurt

1. Prepare Tinga and Corn Salsa.

2. To serve, place one taco shell on each of 6 dinner plates; top equally with lettuce and Tinga. Add salsa and yogurt to taste. Makes 6 servings.

Tinga. Trim and discard fat from 1 pound **beef flank steak;** cut meat into 2-inch chunks. In a 5- to 6-quart pan, combine meat; 2 medium-size **onions,** chopped; 12 cloves **garlic,** minced or pressed; 4 large **dry bay leaves;** 1 **cinnamon stick** (3 inches long); 10 **whole cloves;** 1 teaspoon *each* **dry marjoram** and **dry thyme;** and 6 cups **water.** Bring to a boil over high heat; then reduce heat and simmer, uncovered, until meat is tender when pierced (about 1 hour).

Meanwhile, drain 1 large can (about 28 oz.) **tomatoes** and discard liquid. In a wide frying pan, combine tomatoes; 3½ cups cooked **Turkey Chorizo Sausage,** page 56 (or use purchased chorizo sausage, casings removed, meat crumbled and cooked); 2 medium-size **onions,** chopped; 2 tablespoons (or to taste) **canned chipotle chiles in adobo or adobado sauce,** minced; ¼ cup **cider vinegar;** and 2 tablespoons firmly packed **brown sugar.** Cook over medium-high heat, uncovered, stirring often and breaking tomatoes up, until all liquid has evaporated (about 30 minutes).

When beef is done, transfer it with a slotted spoon to a bowl. Pour cooking liquid into a strainer set over another bowl and press to remove liquid; discard residue. Return liquid to pan and boil over high heat until reduced to 1½ cups. Add liquid to chorizo mixture. Tear beef into shreds; add to chorizo mixture.

Use filling hot or warm. If made ahead, cover and refrigerate for up to 3 days. Reheat before using. Makes about 5 cups.

Per serving: 337 calories (16% calories from fat), 32 g protein, 47 g carbohydrates, 7 g total fat (2 g saturated fat), 62 mg cholesterol, 481 mg sodium

Lemon Shrimp Tostadas

Preparation time: About 15 minutes

Chilling time: At least 20 minutes

Served cold, this light tostada features a topping of shrimp and jicama in a lemon-honey marinade. It's perfect for a hot-weather lunch or supper.

> 1 pound tiny cooked shrimp
>
> 1 cup peeled, finely minced jicama
>
> 3 tablespoons sliced green onions
>
> 1 teaspoon grated lemon peel
>
> 3 tablespoons lemon juice
>
> 2 teaspoons honey
>
> White pepper
>
> About 1½ cups Cherry Tomato Salsa (page 32) or other salsa of your choice
>
> 6 crisp corn taco shells (page 25) or warm corn tortillas (page 25)
>
> 3 cups shredded lettuce
>
> 1 medium-size firm-ripe tomato (about 6 oz.), finely chopped

1. In a nonmetal bowl, mix shrimp, jicama, onions, lemon peel, lemon juice, and honey; season to taste with white pepper. Cover and refrigerate for at least 20 minutes or up to 3 hours.

2. Meanwhile, prepare Cherry Tomato Salsa and refrigerate.

3. To serve, place one taco shell on each of 6 dinner plates; top equally with lettuce. Scoop out shrimp mixture with a slotted spoon, drain, and divide equally among taco shells. Top equally with tomato. Add salsa to taste. Makes 6 servings.

Per serving: 156 calories (9% calories from fat), 18 g protein, 18 g carbohydrates, 2 g total fat (0.3 g saturated fat), 148 mg cholesterol, 217 mg sodium

TORTILLAS

In Mexican homes, tortillas are enjoyed plain with most meals—sometimes eaten whole, sometimes torn or cut into pieces. And of course, the versatile breads are also stacked, rolled, or folded around all kinds of fillings. Though tortillas are often fried before serving, you can achieve the same crispness—without added fat—by baking or toasting.

Look for packaged fresh corn and flour tortillas in the ethnic section of your supermarket. Once purchased, tortillas can be stored airtight in the refrigerator for up to a week; freeze them for longer storage.

WARM TORTILLAS

6 corn tortillas (6-inch diameter) or flour tortillas (7- to 9-inch diameter)

1. Brush tortillas lightly with hot water; then stack, wrap in foil, and heat in a 350° oven until warm (10 to 12 minutes). Makes 6 tortillas.

Per corn tortilla: 56 calories (10% calories from fat), 1 g protein, 12 g carbohydrates, 0.6 g total fat (0.1 g saturated fat), 0 mg cholesterol, 40 mg sodium

Per flour tortilla: 114 calories (20% calories from fat), 3 g protein, 20 g carbohydrates, 3 g total fat (0.4 g saturated fat), 0 mg cholesterol, 167 mg sodium

CRISP TACO SHELLS

6 corn tortillas (6-inch diameter) or flour tortillas (7- to 9-inch diameter)
Salt (optional)

1. Dip tortillas, one at a time, in hot water; drain briefly. Season to taste with salt, if desired.

2. Arrange tortillas in a single layer on large baking sheets. Do not overlap tortillas. Bake in a 500° oven for 4 minutes. With a metal spatula, turn tortillas over; continue to bake until crisp and browned (about 2 more minutes).

If made ahead, let cool; then store airtight at room temperature for up to 5 days. Makes 6 crisp taco shells (unlike commercial curved taco shells, these are flat shells for open-faced tacos).

Per corn taco shell: 56 calories (10% calories from fat), 1 g protein, 12 g carbohydrates, 0.6 g total fat (0.1 g saturated fat), 0 mg cholesterol, 40 mg sodium

Per flour taco shell: 114 calories (20% calories from fat), 3 g protein, 20 g carbohydrates, 3 g total fat (0.4 g saturated fat), 0 mg cholesterol, 167 mg sodium

WATER-CRISPED TORTILLA CHIPS

6 corn tortillas (6-inch diameter) or flour tortillas (7- to 9-inch diameter)
Salt (optional)

1. Dip tortillas, one at a time, in hot water; drain briefly. Season tortillas to taste with salt, if desired. Stack tortillas; then cut the stack into 6 to 8 wedges.

2. Arrange wedges in a single layer on large baking sheets. Do not overlap wedges. Bake in a 500° oven for 4 minutes. With a metal spatula, turn wedges over; continue to bake until crisp and browned (about 2 more minutes). If made ahead, let cool; then store airtight at room temperature for up to 5 days. Makes about 4 cups corn chips, about 6 cups flour chips.

Per cup of corn chips: 83 calories (10% calories from fat), 2 g protein, 18 g carbohydrates, 1 g total fat (0.1 g saturated fat), 0 mg cholesterol, 60 mg sodium

Per cup of flour chips: 85 calories (20% calories from fat), 2 g protein, 15 g carbohydrates, 2 g total fat (0.3 g saturated fat), 0 mg cholesterol, 126 mg sodium

CRISP CORN TORTILLA STRIPS

3 corn tortillas (6-inch diameter)
Salt (optional)

1. Dip tortillas, one at a time, in hot water; drain briefly. Season to taste with salt, if desired. Stack tortillas; cut stack in half, then cut into ¼-inch-wide strips.

2. Arrange strips in a single layer on a large baking sheet. Do not overlap strips. Bake in a 500° oven for 3 minutes. With a metal spatula, turn strips over and continue to bake until crisp and browned (about 1 more minute). If made ahead, let cool; then store airtight at room temperature for up to 5 days. Makes about 1½ cups.

Per ½ cup: 56 calories (10% calories from fat), 1 g protein, 12 g carbohydrates, 0.6 g total fat (0.1 g saturated fat), 0 mg cholesterol, 40 mg sodium

Start a company meal with warm Picadillo-stuffed Empanadas
(recipe on page 28): tiny, cornmeal-crusted turnovers, plump with a piquant
turkey filling. If you like, accompany the empanadas with a selection
of fresh raw vegetables.

A P P E T I Z E R S

If you're hungry for *antojitos* ("little whims") to enjoy at any time of day, look to the classic and contemporary recipes in this chapter. You'll find plenty of choices, both hot and cold: spicy empanadas, juicy chicken bites, refreshing salsas, luscious guacamole, and more. Select just one dish to introduce a meal, or offer several together for a light lunch or supper.

Pictured on page 26

Picadillo-stuffed Empanadas

Preparation time: About 30 minutes

Cooking time: About 1¼ hours

Ground meat and onions simmered in a savory-sweet tomato sauce make *picadillo,* a satisfying filling for bite-size turnovers. Serve these little pastries as appetizers or enjoy them as an anytime snack.

        Cornmeal-Cumin Pastry (recipe follows)
- 2 **tablespoons slivered almonds**
- 1 **teaspoon salad oil**
- 1 **large onion, finely chopped**
- 2 **cloves garlic, minced or pressed**
- 6 **ounces ground turkey or chicken breast**
- 1 **can (about 8 oz.) tomato sauce**
- ½ **teaspoon ground cinnamon**
- ⅛ **teaspoon ground cloves**
- 2 **tablespoons dried currants or raisins**
- 2 **teaspoons cider vinegar**
    Salt

1. Prepare Cornmeal-Cumin Pastry.

2. Toast almonds in a small frying pan over medium heat until golden (5 to 7 minutes), stirring often. Transfer almonds to a bowl and let cool; then coarsely chop and set aside.

3. In a wide nonstick frying pan, combine oil, onion, garlic, and 1 tablespoon water. Cook over medium heat, stirring often, until mixture is deep golden (about 20 minutes); if onion sticks to pan bottom or pan appears dry, add more water, 1 tablespoon at a time. Crumble turkey into pan and cook over medium-high heat, stirring often, until well browned (about 10 minutes); if pan appears dry, add more water, 1 tablespoon at a time.

4. Stir in tomato sauce, cinnamon, cloves, and currants. Bring mixture to a boil; then reduce heat and simmer, uncovered, until almost all liquid has evaporated and mixture is slightly thickened (about 10 minutes). Remove from heat, stir in almonds and vinegar, and season to taste with salt.

5. On a floured board, roll out pastry ⅛ inch thick. Cut into 3½-inch rounds. Spoon equal amounts of turkey filling onto half of each pastry round. Moisten edges of rounds with water; fold plain half of each round over filling. Press edges together with a fork.

6. Arrange empanadas on a lightly oiled 12- by 15-inch baking sheet. Bake in a 400° oven until lightly browned (about 20 minutes). Makes about 16 empanadas.

Cornmeal-Cumin Pastry. In a food processor (or a bowl), combine 1 cup **all-purpose flour,** ½ cup **yellow cornmeal,** 1½ teaspoons **baking powder,** ¼ teaspoon **salt,** and 2 tablespoons **butter** or margarine. Whirl (or rub with your fingers) until mixture resembles coarse crumbs. Add ⅓ cup **milk,** 1 large **egg white,** and ½ teaspoon **cumin seeds;** whirl (or stir with a fork) until dough holds together (add 1 more tablespoon **milk,** if needed). With lightly floured hands, pat dough into a ball. Wrap airtight and refrigerate until ready to use or for up to 1 hour.

Per empanada: 96 calories (26% calories from fat), 5 g protein, 13 g carbohydrates, 3 g total fat (1 g saturated fat), 11 mg cholesterol, 192 mg sodium

Watermelon, Jicama & Chili Salt

Preparation time: About 10 minutes

Crisp watermelon wedges and jicama slices are seasoned with lemon, chili, and salt for a quick appetizer.

- 4 **seedless or seed-in watermelon wedges (4 to 5 lbs. *total*), *each* about 3 inches wide and 9 inches long**
    About 1¼ pounds jicama, peeled and rinsed
- ½ **teaspoon *each* salt and ground red pepper (cayenne)**
- 1 **lemon, cut into quarters**

1. Slide a short, sharp knife between rind and flesh of watermelon wedges to free flesh, but keep flesh in place. Then cut through melon to rind at 1½-inch intervals.

2. Cut jicama into ¼-inch-thick slices, each about 2 by 3 inches. Insert jicama slices in melon slits.

3. Mix salt and red pepper; sprinkle over melon and jicama. Serve with lemon quarters to squeeze over fruit to taste. Makes 4 servings.

Per serving: 145 calories (8% calories from fat), 4 g protein, 34 g carbohydrates, 2 g total fat (0 g saturated fat), 0 mg cholesterol, 287 mg sodium

Tomato-Crab Quesadillas

Preparation time: About 15 minutes

Cooking time: 20 to 30 minutes

Warm crab, tomatoes, and jack cheese make a great filling for quesadillas. Offer a cool fresh-chile sauce to heat up each serving.

Chile Sauce (recipe follows)
2 medium-size firm-ripe tomatoes (about 12 oz. *total*), finely chopped
4 ounces cooked crabmeat
¾ cup shredded jack cheese
1 cup sliced green onions
10 flour tortillas (7- to 9-inch diameter)
Cilantro sprigs

1. Prepare Chile Sauce and set aside.

2. Place tomatoes in a fine wire strainer and let drain well; discard juice.

3. In a bowl, mix crab, cheese, and onions. Gently mix in tomatoes. Place 5 tortillas in a single layer on 2 lightly oiled large baking sheets. Evenly top tortillas with crab mixture, covering tortillas to within ¾ inch of edges. Top each tortilla with one of the remaining tortillas.

4. Bake in a 450° oven until tortillas are lightly browned (7 to 9 minutes), switching positions of baking sheets halfway through baking.

5. Slide quesadillas onto a serving board; cut each into 6 wedges. Garnish with cilantro sprigs. Add Chile Sauce to taste. Makes 8 to 10 servings.

Chile Sauce. Place 4 medium-size **fresh green Anaheim chiles** or other large mild chiles (about 7 oz. *total*) on a baking sheet. Broil 4 to 6 inches below heat, turning often, until charred all over (about 8 minutes). Cover with foil and let cool on baking sheet; then remove and discard skins, stems, and seeds.

In a blender or food processor, whirl chiles, ¼ cup **dry white wine,** 2 small **shallots,** and 1 tablespoon **lemon juice** until smooth. Pour into a 2- to 3-quart pan. Bring to a boil; boil, stirring, until reduced to ⅓ cup (5 to 10 minutes).

Return mixture to blender or food processor. Add 1 cup firmly packed **cilantro leaves** and ½ cup peeled, coarsely chopped **jicama.** Whirl until smooth; scrape sides of container several times. With motor running, slowly add ¼ cup **low-sodi-um chicken broth** and 1 tablespoon **honey** and whirl to blend. Serve sauce cool or cold. If made ahead, cover and refrigerate for up to 4 hours. Makes about 1 cup.

Per serving: 182 calories (27% calories from fat), 8 g protein, 24 g carbohydrates, 5 g total fat (0.4 g saturated fat), 19 mg cholesterol, 277 mg sodium

Pictured on front cover

Creamy Guacamole

Preparation time: About 10 minutes

Guacamole is offered as a condiment at many Mexican meals—and enjoyed as a snack, too. To make this creamy, reduced-fat version of the popular dip, we used a ripe avocado for flavor, but cut the fat by adding cottage cheese.

1 teaspoon grated lemon peel
2 tablespoons lemon juice
1 medium-size soft-ripe avocado
1 cup lowfat (1%) cottage cheese
2 to 4 cloves garlic, peeled
⅛ teaspoon salt
2 tablespoons minced cilantro
1 fresh jalapeño or serrano chile, seeded and minced
1 tablespoon thinly sliced green onion
2 small tomatoes (about 8 oz. *total*), finely chopped and drained well
Cilantro sprigs
About 8 cups water-crisped corn tortilla chips (page 25), purchased tortilla chips, or bite-size pieces of raw vegetables

1. Place lemon peel and lemon juice in a blender or food processor. Pit and peel avocado; transfer avocado to blender along with cottage cheese, garlic, and salt. Whirl until smoothly puréed.

2. Spoon guacamole into a serving bowl and gently stir in minced cilantro, chile, onion, and half the tomatoes. If made ahead, cover and refrigerate for up to 2 hours; stir before serving.

3. To serve, garnish with remaining tomatoes and cilantro sprigs. To eat, scoop guacamole onto chips. Makes about 3 cups (about 8 servings).

Per serving (including chips): 138 calories (23% calories from fat), 6 g protein, 22 g carbohydrates, 4 g total fat (0.7 g saturated fat), 1 mg cholesterol, 215 mg sodium

Turkey Jerky

Preparation time: About 10 minutes

Marinating time: At least 1 hour

Baking time: 4 to 6 hours (in a conventional oven)

For a lowfat appetizer or snack, chewy jerky made from turkey breast is a tasty choice. For the liveliest flavor, let the turkey strips marinate for the maximum time.

- 1 **pound skinless, boneless turkey breast; or 1 pound turkey breast tenderloins**
- 1 **tablespoon salt**
- ½ **cup water**
- 2 **tablespoons firmly packed brown sugar**
- 2 **cloves garlic, minced or pressed; or ¼ teaspoon garlic powder**
- ½ **small onion, minced; or ¼ teaspoon onion powder**
- 1 **teaspoon pepper**
- ½ **teaspoon liquid smoke**
  Vegetable oil cooking spray

1. Rinse turkey and pat dry. Pull off and discard any fat and connective tissue. For easier slicing, freeze meat until it's firm but not hard. Cut into ⅛- to ¼-inch-thick slices (cut breast piece with or across the grain, tenderloins lengthwise).

2. In a nonmetal bowl, stir together salt, water, sugar, garlic, onion, pepper, and liquid smoke. Add turkey and mix well. Cover and refrigerate for at least 1 hour or up to 24 hours; turkey will absorb almost all liquid.

3. You may dry turkey in a dehydrator or a conventional oven. Depending upon drying method, evenly coat dehydrator racks (you need 3, each about 10 by 13 inches) or metal racks (to cover a 10- by 15-inch rimmed baking pan) with cooking spray. Lift turkey strips from bowl and shake off any excess liquid; lay strips close together, but not overlapping, on racks.

4. If using a dehydrator, arrange trays as manufacturer directs and dry at 140° until jerky cracks and breaks when bent (4½ to 6 hours; remove a strip of jerky from dehydrator and let stand for about 5 minutes before testing).

If using an oven, place pan on center rack of a 150° to 200° oven; prop door open about 2 inches.

Dry until jerky cracks and breaks when bent (4 to 6 hours; remove a strip of jerky from oven and let stand for about 5 minutes before testing).

5. Let jerky cool on racks. Serve; or package airtight and store in a cool, dry place for up to 3 weeks, in the refrigerator for up to 4 months (freeze for longer storage). Makes about 7 ounces.

Per ounce: 93 calories (8% calories from fat), 16 g protein, 5 g carbohydrates, 1 g total fat (0.1 g saturated fat), 40 mg cholesterol, 975 mg sodium

Pictured on facing page

Garlic Chicken Bites with Tomato-Raisin Sauce

Preparation time: About 10 minutes

Baking time: 18 to 20 minutes

Serve these tender, garlicky chunks of skinless chicken hot from the oven, with a spicy-sweet tomato-raisin sauce.

- 3 **tablespoons minced cilantro**
- 2 **teaspoons coarsely ground pepper**
- 8 **cloves garlic, minced**
- 1 **pound skinless, boneless chicken thighs, cut into 1½-inch chunks**
- ⅓ **cup tomato sauce**
- 1 **tablespoon firmly packed brown sugar**
- 1 **tablespoon distilled white vinegar or cider vinegar**
- ½ **cup raisins**

1. Mix cilantro, pepper, and 6 cloves of the garlic; rub mixture over chicken. Place chicken pieces well apart in a lightly oiled 10- by 15-inch rimmed baking pan.

2. Bake in a 500° oven until chicken is lightly browned and no longer pink in center; cut to test (18 to 20 minutes).

3. Meanwhile, in a food processor or blender, whirl remaining 2 cloves garlic, tomato sauce, sugar, vinegar, and raisins until raisins are chopped.

4. Serve chicken hot, with tomato-raisin sauce. Makes 4 servings.

Per serving: 221 calories (19% calories from fat), 24 g protein, 22 g carbohydrates, 5 g total fat (1 g saturated fat), 94 mg cholesterol, 224 mg sodium

Coated with garlic, black pepper, and cilantro, these sizzling-hot Garlic Chicken Bites (recipe on facing page) are ready to enjoy with sweet-tart Tomato-Raisin Sauce. Icy-cold margaritas temper the chicken's spicy heat.

31

S A L S A S

In Mexico, colorful fresh or cooked salsas are served with virtually every meal. Their flavors ranging from spicy-hot to mildly sweet, these lively condiments are enjoyed as both sauces and dips.

The salsas we present on these pages add a wonderful, fresh-tasting accent to almost any dish. They're great for guilt-free snacking, too; just pair them with homemade corn or flour tortilla chips (see page 25) or assorted crisp raw vegetables and fruits.

CHERRY TOMATO SALSA

For the very best flavor, use fully ripe, juicy tomatoes in this mild salsa.

- 2 cups (about 12 oz.) red cherry tomatoes, cut into halves
- ⅓ cup lightly packed cilantro leaves
- 2 fresh jalapeño chiles, seeded
- 1 clove garlic, peeled
- 2 tablespoons *each* lime juice and thinly sliced green onion
  Salt and pepper

1. Place tomatoes, cilantro, chiles, and garlic in a food processor; whirl just until coarsely chopped (or chop coarsely with a knife).

2. Turn mixture into a nonmetal bowl; stir in lime juice and onion. Season to taste with salt and pepper. If made ahead, cover and refrigerate for up to 4 hours. Makes about 2 cups.

Per ¼ cup: 12 calories (8% calories from fat), 0.4 g protein, 0.1 g carbohydrates, 2 g total fat (0 g saturated fat), 0 mg cholesterol, 5 mg sodium

SPICY PEPPER RELISH

No need to worry about this sweet-hot relish wilting—it's cooked, so it holds well in the refrigerator for up to 3 days. Try it with grilled meats, fish, or poultry.

- 2 large red bell peppers (about 1 lb. *total*)
- 2 large yellow bell peppers (about 1 lb. *total*)
- 8 fresh red or green serrano chiles (about 2 oz. *total*)
- 1 cup sugar
- ⅔ cup distilled white vinegar

1. Seed bell peppers and chiles; cut into thin strips. In a large bowl, mix peppers, chiles, sugar, and vinegar; pour into a wide frying pan.

2. Place pan over medium to medium-high heat. Cook, uncovered, stirring often, until almost all liquid has evaporated (about 30 minutes). Let cool slightly before serving. If made ahead, cover and refrigerate for up to 3 days. Makes about 1½ cups.

Per ¼ cup: 168 calories (1% calories from fat), 1 g protein, 43 g carbohydrates, 0.2 g total fat (0 g saturated fat), 0 mg cholesterol, 4 mg sodium

CUCUMBER & JICAMA SALSA

Crisp and fresh, this pale green-and-white salsa is best if served within a few hours after it's made.

- 1 medium-size cucumber (about 8 oz.), peeled, seeded, and diced
  About 1 pound jicama, peeled, rinsed, and diced
- ⅓ cup *each* chopped fresh basil and sliced green onions
- ¼ cup *each* lemon juice and plain nonfat yogurt
- 1 small fresh jalapeño chile, seeded and minced
  Salt

1. In a nonmetal bowl, mix cucumber, jicama, basil, onions, lemon juice, yogurt, and chile; season to taste with salt. If made ahead, cover and refrigerate for up to 6 hours. Makes about 6 cups.

Per ¼ cup: 11 calories (3% calories from fat), 0.5 g protein, 2 g carbohydrates, 0.1 g total fat (0 g saturated fat), 0.1 mg cholesterol, 4 mg sodium

CORN SALSA

Enjoy the season's best fresh corn in a sweet-tangy salsa flavored with orange, chile, and mint.

- 3 medium-size ears corn (about 1½ lbs. *total*), *each* about 8 inches long, husks and silk removed
- ½ cup finely chopped European cucumber
- ⅓ cup lime juice
- ¼ cup thinly sliced green onions
- 1 tablespoon grated orange peel
- 3 tablespoons orange juice
- 2 tablespoons chopped fresh mint or 1 teaspoon dry mint
- 1 teaspoon cumin seeds
- 1 or 2 fresh jalapeño chiles, seeded and minced
  Salt

1. In a 5- to 6-quart pan, bring about 3 quarts water to a boil over high heat. Add corn, cover, and cook until hot (4 to 6 minutes). Drain; then let cool. With a sharp knife, cut kernels from cobs.

2. In a nonmetal bowl, mix corn, cucumber, lime juice, onions, orange peel, orange juice, mint, cumin seeds, and chiles; season to taste with salt. If made ahead, cover and refrigerate for up to 4 hours. Makes about 3 cups.

Per ¼ cup: 32 calories (9% calories from fat), 1 g protein, 7 g carbohydrates, 0.4 g total fat (0.1 g saturated fat), 0 mg cholesterol, 6 mg sodium

PAPAYA SALSA

When you choose papayas for this salsa, select fruit that's about as soft as a ripe peach, with more yellow than green in the skin. (If you use Mexican papayas, however, keep in mind that the fruit may remain mostly green even when fully ripe.)

- 1 medium-size firm-ripe papaya (about 1 lb.), peeled, seeded, and cut into ¼-inch cubes
- ¼ cup chopped cilantro
- 3 green onions, thinly sliced
- 1 fresh jalapeño chile, seeded and minced
- 2 tablespoons lime juice

1. In a nonmetal bowl, gently mix papaya, cilantro, onions, chile, and lime juice. If made ahead, cover and refrigerate for up to 4 hours. Makes about 2 cups.

Per ¼ cup: 18 calories (3% calories from fat), 0.4 g protein, 5 g carbohydrates, 0.1 g total fat (0 g saturated fat), 0 mg cholesterol, 3 mg sodium

WATERMELON PICO DE GALLO

There's more than one kind of *pico de gallo* ("rooster's beak"); this pretty version is made with orange, watermelon, and jicama.

- 1 medium-large orange (about 8 oz.)
- 1½ cups seeded, diced watermelon
- ¾ cup peeled, diced jicama
- 1 fresh jalapeño chile, seeded and minced
- 1 tablespoon *each* lime juice and minced cilantro

1. Finely grate 2 teaspoons peel (colored part only) from orange; place in a nonmetal bowl.

2. Cut off remaining peel and all white membrane from orange. Holding fruit over bowl to catch juice, cut between membranes to release orange segments; then dice segments and drop into bowl.

3. Add watermelon, jicama, chile, lime juice, and cilantro to bowl; mix gently. If made ahead, cover and refrigerate for up to 4 hours. Makes about 3 cups.

Per ¼ cup: 17 calories (4% calories from fat), 0.3 g protein, 4 g carbohydrates, 0.1 g total fat (0 g saturated fat), 0 mg cholesterol, 1 mg sodium

Pictured on front cover

LIME SALSA

Tomatillos and fresh lime make a marvelously tart salsa. Look for firm, smooth tomatillos; before using them, remove the papery husks and rinse off the sticky coating.

- 1 large ripe red or yellow tomato (about 8 oz.), finely diced
- 8 medium-size tomatillos (about 8 oz. *total*), husked, rinsed, and chopped
- ¼ cup minced red or yellow bell pepper
- 2 tablespoons minced red onion
- 1 teaspoon grated lime peel
- 1 tablespoon lime juice

1. In a nonmetal bowl, mix tomato, tomatillos, bell pepper, onion, lime peel, and lime juice. If made ahead, cover and refrigerate for up to 4 hours. Makes about 4 cups.

Per ¼ cup: 7 calories (9% calories from fat), 0.3 g protein, 1 g carbohydrates, 0.1 g total fat (0 g saturated fat), 0 mg cholesterol, 2 mg sodium

PINEAPPLE SALSA

Cool and refreshing, this salsa is delicious with shellfish, fajitas, or just plain chips.

- 1 cup diced fresh or canned pineapple
- ½ cup chopped peeled, seeded cucumber
- 1 fresh jalapeño chile, seeded and minced
- 1 teaspoon grated lime peel
- 3 tablespoons lime juice
- 2 tablespoons minced cilantro

1. In a nonmetal bowl, mix pineapple, cucumber, chile, lime peel, lime juice, and cilantro. If made ahead, cover and refrigerate for up to 4 hours. Makes about 1¾ cups.

Per ¼ cup: 14 calories (5% calories from fat), 0.2 g protein, 4 g carbohydrates, 0.1 g total fat (0 g saturated fat), 0 mg cholesterol, 2 mg sodium

Fresh-tasting Turkey Albondigas Soup (recipe on page 36) is a Mexican favorite that's just right for a warming autumn supper. Offer homemade Cornhusk Muffins (recipe on page 93) alongside.

S O U P S

S A L A D S

Piping hot or refreshingly chilly, savory soups

awaken appetites. Serve them as a first course, as

Mexican cooks often do; or make a light meal by

adding warm tortillas and one of our salads. Pair

cool Curried Corn Shrimp Soup with greens or

crisp Cilantro Slaw; complement hearty Pozole with

a colorful fresh-fruit "salsa."

Black Bean Soup

Preparation time: About 10 minutes

Cooking time: About 30 minutes

Mexican cooks use nourishing, earthy-tasting black beans in a variety of dishes. To make this satisfying soup, you can use home-cooked dried beans if you like—but we suggest you speed up preparation with the canned or instant refried variety. (Refried bean mix is sold in natural-foods stores and some well-stocked supermarkets.)

> 2 teaspoons salad oil
> 1 large onion, chopped
> 1¾ or 2¾ cups low-sodium chicken broth
> 1 large can (about 28 oz.) tomatoes
> 3 cans (about 15 oz. *each*) black beans, drained, rinsed, and puréed; or 1 package (about 7 oz.) instant refried black bean mix
> 1 fresh jalapeño chile, seeded and minced
> 2 teaspoons cumin seeds
> Condiments (suggestions follow)

1. In a 5- to 6-quart pan, combine oil and onion. Cook over medium heat, stirring often, until onion is deep golden (about 20 minutes). Add 1¾ cups broth (or 2¾ cups if using instant beans).

2. Add tomatoes and their liquid to pan; break tomatoes up with a spoon. Stir in beans, chile, and cumin seeds. Bring to a boil; then reduce heat and simmer, uncovered, until soup is thick and flavors are blended (7 to 10 minutes).

3. To serve, ladle soup into bowls. Add condiments to taste. Makes 4 servings.

Condiments. Offer in individual bowls: shredded **Cheddar cheese, plain nonfat yogurt, cilantro leaves, lime wedges,** and **water-crisped tortilla chips** (page 25).

Per serving: 331 calories (15% calories from fat), 21 g protein, 51 g carbohydrates, 6 g total fat (0.7 g saturated fat), 0 mg cholesterol, 757 mg sodium

Pictured on page 34

Turkey Albondigas Soup

Preparation time: About 30 minutes

Cooking time: About 15 minutes

This flavorful and nutritious meal-in-a-bowl features turkey meatballs, tomatoes, carrots, and spinach in a light broth. If you like, you can make the meatballs a day ahead.

> Turkey Meatballs (recipe follows)
> 1 can (about 14½ oz.) pear-shaped tomatoes
> 6 cups low-sodium chicken broth
> 4 cups beef broth
> 2 cups chopped onions
> 6 medium-size carrots (about 1½ lbs. *total*), thinly sliced
> 1 teaspoon dry oregano
> 2 teaspoons chili powder
> 12 ounces stemmed spinach leaves, rinsed well and drained (about 3 cups lightly packed)
> ⅓ cup chopped cilantro
> 1 or 2 limes, cut into wedges

1. Prepare Turkey Meatballs; set aside.

2. Pour tomatoes and their liquid into an 8- to 10-quart pan; break tomatoes up with a spoon. Add chicken broth, beef broth, onions, carrots, oregano, and chili powder.

3. Bring to a boil over high heat; then reduce heat to low. Add meatballs and simmer for 10 minutes. Stir in spinach and cilantro and cook until greens are wilted (about 3 more minutes).

4. To serve, ladle soup into bowls; serve with lime wedges. Makes 6 to 8 servings.

Turkey Meatballs. In a bowl, mix 1 pound **ground turkey,** ½ cup **cooked brown or white rice,** ¼ cup *each* **all-purpose flour** and **water,** and 1 teaspoon **ground cumin.** Shape mixture into 1- to 1½-inch balls and place, slightly apart, in a 10- by 15-inch rimmed baking pan. Bake in a 450° oven until well browned (about 15 minutes). Pour off fat. If made ahead, let cool; then cover and refrigerate until next day.

Per serving: 247 calories (25% calories from fat), 19 g protein, 29 g carbohydrates, 7 g total fat (2 g saturated fat), 47 mg cholesterol, 292 mg sodium

Curried Corn Shrimp Soup

Preparation time: About 15 minutes

Cooking time: About 30 minutes

Chilling time: At least 3 hours

A full quart of buttermilk adds low-calorie nutrition, an interesting sharp flavor, and a smooth, creamy texture to this warm-weather soup. The soup takes only minutes to prepare, but it does need time to chill.

- 2 cups low-sodium chicken broth
- 2 large tart apples (about 1 lb. *total*), peeled, cored, and chopped
- 1 large onion, chopped
- ½ teaspoon curry powder
- 1 large red bell pepper (about 8 oz.)
- 4 cups cold buttermilk
- ¼ cup lime juice
- 1½ cups cooked yellow or white corn kernels (from 2 medium-size ears corn); or 1 package (about 10 oz.) frozen corn kernels, drained
- ½ cup minced cilantro
- ⅓ pound tiny cooked shrimp
  Cilantro sprigs

1. In a 4- to 5-quart pan, combine broth, apples, onion, and curry powder. Bring to a boil over high heat; then reduce heat, cover, and simmer until apples mash easily (about 30 minutes).

2. Let cool; then cover and refrigerate until cold (at least 3 hours) or until next day. Pour mixture into a blender or food processor and whirl until smoothly puréed.

3. Seed bell pepper and cut a few thin slivers from it; set slivers aside. Dice remaining pepper. Put diced pepper in a tureen and stir in apple-onion purée, buttermilk, lime juice, 1¼ cups of the corn, and minced cilantro. (At this point, you may cover and refrigerate soup, pepper slivers, and remaining ¼ cup corn until next day.)

4. To serve, ladle soup into bowls and top equally with shrimp, remaining corn, bell pepper slivers, and cilantro sprigs. Makes 6 servings.

Per serving: 213 calories (12% calories from fat), 14 g protein, 36 g carbohydrates, 3 g total fat (1 g saturated fat), 55 mg cholesterol, 257 mg sodium

Chilled Cucumber & Cilantro Soup

Preparation time: About 10 minutes

Chilling time: At least 2 hours

Here's a cool no-cook soup that's perfect for hot days. Just purée cucumber and cilantro with broth and a little nonfat milk, then chill the soup to let the flavors mingle.

- 1 very large cucumber (about 1 lb.), peeled and cut into chunks
- 1¼ cups low-sodium chicken broth
- ¾ cup firmly packed cilantro leaves
- ½ cup nonfat or lowfat milk
- ¼ cup lemon juice
  Salt

1. In a food processor or blender, combine cucumber, broth, cilantro, milk, and lemon juice; whirl until smoothly puréed. Season purée to taste with salt.

2. Cover and refrigerate until cold (at least 2 hours) or until next day.

3. To serve, ladle into bowls. Makes 4 servings.

Per serving: 38 calories (15% calories from fat), 3 g protein, 6 g carbohydrates, 0.7 g total fat (0.2 g saturated fat), 0.6 mg cholesterol, 43 mg sodium

GAZPACHO

The original gazpacho, created in the southern Spanish region of Andalusia, consisted of bread pounded with olive oil and seasoned with garlic, almonds, and vinegar. Today, though, you'll find all kinds of gazpachos, many featuring tomatoes as well as other fruits and vegetables. When the weather sizzles, these refreshing soups are delightful for lunch or supper.

Pictured on facing page
WHITE GAZPACHO

This mild soup is easy to prepare, yet elegant enough for a party menu.

- 1 European cucumber (about 1 lb.), peeled and coarsely chopped
- 2 cups plain nonfat yogurt
- 2 tablespoons lemon juice
- 1 clove garlic, peeled
- 2 cups low-sodium chicken broth
- 2 tablespoons minced cilantro
- 2 tablespoons sliced green onion
  Thin cucumber slices
  Thinly slivered green onion tops

1. In a blender or food processor, whirl chopped cucumber, yogurt, lemon juice, and garlic until smoothly puréed (if using a blender, also add about ½ cup of the broth). Pour purée into a 2-quart container and stir in broth.

2. Cover and refrigerate until cold (at least 2 hours) or until next day. Then stir in cilantro and sliced onion.

3. Pour mixture into a nonmetal serving bowl or pitcher. To serve, ladle or pour into bowls or glasses; garnish with cucumber slices and slivered onion. Makes 4 servings.

Per serving: 103 calories (9% calories from fat), 9 g protein, 15 g carbohydrates, 1 g total fat (0.4 g saturated fat), 2 mg cholesterol, 125 mg sodium

TOMATO & ROASTED PEPPER GAZPACHO

Sweet peppers, tomatoes, and lime mingle in this robust gazpacho.

- 3 medium-size red bell peppers (about 1¼ lbs. *total*)
- 1½ cups low-sodium chicken broth
- ¼ cup lime juice
- 3 green onions, thinly sliced
- 3 medium-size firm-ripe pear-shaped (Roma-type) tomatoes (about 8 oz. *total*), diced
- 1 *each* small yellow and green bell pepper (about ⅓ lb. *each*), seeded and diced
  Salt and pepper

1. Cut red bell peppers in half lengthwise. Set halves, cut side down, in a 10- by 15-inch rimmed baking pan. Broil 4 to 6 inches below heat until charred all over (about 8 minutes). Cover with foil and let cool in pan. Remove and discard skins, stems, and seeds.

2. In a food processor or blender, whirl roasted peppers, broth, and lime juice until smoothly puréed.

Stir in onions, tomatoes, and yellow and green bell peppers; season to taste with salt and pepper.

3. Cover and refrigerate until cold (at least 2 hours) or until next day. Makes 4 servings.

Per serving: 78 calories (11% calories from fat), 3 g protein, 16 g carbohydrates, 1 g total fat (0.2 g saturated fat), 0 mg cholesterol, 33 mg sodium

GOLDEN TOMATO-PAPAYA GAZPACHO

Here's an unusual gazpacho based on yellow tomatoes and papaya.

- 2 pounds ripe yellow regular or cherry tomatoes
- 1 large ripe papaya (about 1¼ lbs.), peeled, seeded, and diced
- 1 cup diced cucumber
- ¼ cup minced onion
- 2 tablespoons white wine vinegar
- 2 cups low-sodium chicken broth
- 2 tablespoons minced fresh basil
- ⅛ teaspoon liquid hot pepper seasoning
  Salt
  Basil sprigs

1. Dice tomatoes; place in a large nonmetal bowl. Stir in papaya, cucumber, onion, vinegar, broth, minced basil, and hot pepper seasoning. Season to taste with salt.

2. Cover and refrigerate until cold (at least 2 hours) or until next day. Garnish with basil sprigs. Makes 10 to 12 servings.

Per serving: 38 calories (12% calories from fat), 1 g protein, 8 g carbohydrates, 1 g total fat (0.1 g saturated fat), 0 mg cholesterol, 19 mg sodium

*Garnished with thin cucumber slices and strands of green onion,
creamy White Gazpacho (recipe on facing page) is a snap to assemble
and serve. Fresh rolls and iced tea nicely complement the chilled
cucumber-yogurt soup.*

Pozole

Preparation time: About 15 minutes

Cooking time: About 1¾ hours

Pozole is a pork, chicken, and hominy soup that's a favorite throughout Mexico. The recipe varies from place to place; as you travel across the country, you'll notice slight variations in ingredients and seasonings. Our pozole calls for canned hominy, but if you like, you can substitute the dried or partially cooked frozen hominy sold at Mexican markets.

> 1 **pound pork tenderloin, trimmed of fat and silvery membrane and cut into 1½-inch chunks**
> 1 **pound skinless, boneless chicken or turkey thighs, cut into 1½-inch chunks**
> 3 **quarts low-sodium chicken broth**
> 2 **large onions, cut into chunks**
> 1 **teaspoon dry oregano**
> ½ **teaspoon cumin seeds**
> 2 **cans (about 14 oz. *each*) yellow hominy, drained**
> **Salt and pepper**
> **Lime slices or wedges**
> 1½ **cups crisp corn tortilla strips (page 25)**

1. Place pork and chicken in a 6- to 8-quart pan. Add broth, onions, oregano, and cumin seeds to pan. Bring to a boil over high heat; then reduce heat, cover, and simmer until meat is tender when pierced (about 1½ hours). Lift out meat with a slotted spoon; place in a bowl to cool.

2. Pour cooking broth into a strainer set over a bowl. Press residue to remove liquid; discard residue. Return broth to pan and bring to a boil over high heat.

3. Add hominy and reduce heat; simmer, uncovered, until flavors are blended (about 10 minutes). Coarsely shred meat and return to broth. Serve soup hot or warm. If made ahead, let cool; then cover and refrigerate until next day. Reheat before serving.

4. To serve, ladle into bowls. Season to taste with salt and pepper and serve with lime slices and tortilla strips. Makes 8 to 10 servings.

Per serving: 255 calories (23% calories from fat), 26 g protein, 22 g carbohydrates, 6 g total fat (2 g saturated fat), 75 mg cholesterol, 336 mg sodium

---

Pictured on page 7

Golden Pepper Bisque

Preparation time: About 15 minutes

Cooking time: About 50 minutes

Yellow peppers and carrots give this soup its golden hue; potatoes lend silkiness to the texture. Complete each serving with a drizzle of olive oil, a little *cotija* cheese, and a few croutons.

> **Garlic Croutons (page 48)**
> 2 **large yellow bell peppers (about 1 lb. *total*)**
> 1 **tablespoon salad oil or olive oil**
> 1 **large onion, chopped**
> 2 **large thin-skinned potatoes (about 1 lb. *total*), peeled and cut into ½-inch chunks**
> 2 **large carrots (about ¾ lb. *total*), cut into ½-inch-thick slices**
> 1 **large stalk celery, thinly sliced**
> 6 **cups low-sodium chicken broth**
> **Extra-virgin olive oil**
> **Salt and pepper**
> **Shredded cotija or Parmesan cheese**

1. Prepare Garlic Croutons; set aside.

2. Cut bell peppers in half lengthwise. Set halves, cut side down, in a 10- by 15-inch rimmed baking pan. Broil 4 to 6 inches below heat until charred all over (about 8 minutes). Cover with foil and let cool in pan. Remove and discard skins, stems, and seeds; cut peppers into chunks.

3. In a 5- to 6-quart pan, combine salad oil and onion. Cook over medium-high heat, stirring occasionally, until onion is lightly browned (about 10 minutes). Add roasted bell peppers, potatoes, carrots, celery, and broth. Bring to a boil; then reduce heat, cover, and simmer until carrots are very soft to bite (20 to 25 minutes).

4. In a blender or food processor, whirl vegetable mixture, a portion at a time, until smoothly puréed. If made ahead, let cool; then cover and refrigerate until next day. Reheat, covered, before serving.

5. To serve, ladle soup into wide bowls. Add olive oil, salt, pepper, cheese, and Garlic Croutons to taste. Makes 6 to 8 servings.

Per serving: 137 calories (23% calories from fat), 4 g protein, 23 g carbohydrates, 4 g total fat (0.6 g saturated fat), 0 mg cholesterol, 74 mg sodium

LOWFAT DRESSINGS

Light salad dressings aren't hard to make. Just base them on ingredients that are flavorful, yet virtually fat-free: vinegar, citrus juices, nonfat yogurt, or puréed chiles and herbs. The following four choices are delicious with greens, and just as good on vegetables or grilled meats.

RED CHILE DRESSING

Dried red chiles lend body, color, and heat to this oil-free dressing.

- 3 large dried red New Mexico or California chiles (about ¾ oz. total)
- ¾ cup water
- 6 tablespoons cider vinegar
- 2 tablespoons sugar
- 1 tablespoon chopped fresh ginger

1. Remove and discard stems and most of seeds from chiles. Rinse chiles and cut into ½-inch strips with scissors. In a 1- to 1½-quart pan, combine chiles and water. Bring to a boil. Remove pan from heat; let chiles soak until slightly softened (about 5 minutes).

2. In a blender or food processor, combine chile mixture, vinegar, sugar, and ginger; whirl until smoothly puréed. If made ahead, let cool; then cover and refrigerate for up to 1 week. Makes about 1 cup.

Per tablespoon: 11 calories (15% calories from fat), 0.2 g protein, 3 g carbohydrates, 0.2 g total fat (0 g saturated fat), 0 mg cholesterol, 0.5 mg sodium

GREEN CHILE DRESSING

Fresh lime juice and two kinds of chiles go into a tart dressing that's great with simply cooked vegetables.

- 1 small can (about 4 oz.) diced green chiles
- ⅓ cup lime juice
- ¼ cup *each* water and chopped cilantro
- 1 clove garlic, peeled
- 1 or 2 fresh jalapeño chiles, seeded and chopped
- 1½ teaspoons sugar

1. In a blender or food processor, combine green chiles, lime juice, water, cilantro, garlic, jalapeño chiles, and sugar; whirl until smoothly puréed. If made ahead, cover and refrigerate for up to 4 hours. Makes about 1 cup.

Per tablespoon: 5 calories (2% calories from fat), 0.1 g protein, 1 g carbohydrates, 0 g total fat (0 g saturated fat), 0 mg cholesterol, 44 mg sodium

CREAMY HERB DRESSING

Mild and slightly sweet, this dressing is appealingly creamy.

- 1 cup plain nonfat yogurt
- 3 tablespoons balsamic vinegar
- 1½ teaspoons chopped fresh oregano or ¼ teaspoon dry oregano
- 1 teaspoon Dijon mustard
- 2 to 3 teaspoons sugar

1. In a nonmetal bowl, mix yogurt, vinegar, oregano, mustard, and sugar. If made ahead, cover and refrigerate for up to 3 days. Makes 1¼ cups.

Per tablespoon: 9 calories (3% calories from fat), 0.6 g protein, 2 g carbohydrates, 0 g total fat (0 g saturated fat), 0.2 mg cholesterol, 16 mg sodium

CITRUS DRESSING

Try this tangy dressing on greens, fruit salads, or grilled poultry.

- 2 teaspoons grated orange peel
- ½ cup orange juice
- 2 tablespoons white wine vinegar or distilled white vinegar
- 2 tablespoons minced fresh basil or 2 teaspoons dry basil
- 1 fresh jalapeño chile, seeded and minced
- 1 tablespoon honey
- 2 teaspoons Dijon mustard
- 1 teaspoon ground cumin
- 2 cloves garlic, pressed

1. In a nonmetal bowl, mix orange peel, orange juice, vinegar, basil, chile, honey, mustard, cumin, and garlic. If made ahead, cover and refrigerate for up to 4 hours. Makes ¾ cup.

Per tablespoon: 14 calories (5% calories from fat), 0.2 g protein, 3 g carbohydrates, 0.1 g total fat (0 g saturated fat), 0 mg cholesterol, 26 mg sodium

Cool off a hot day or a spicy meal with refreshing Melon & Cucumber Salad-Salsa (recipe on facing page). Sweet ripe cantaloupe, papaya, and crisp cucumber are tossed with honey and lime juice, then served in individual melon "bowls."

Pictured on page 18

Pickled Vegetables

Preparation time: *About 15 minutes*

Cooking time: *About 15 minutes*

Marinating time: *At least 12 hours*

Known in Mexico as vegetables *en escabeche*, this colorful combination of pickled carrots, chiles, and onion is a superb condiment for fajitas or sandwiches.

> 5 cloves garlic, peeled
>
> 2 medium-size carrots (about 8 oz. *total*), cut into ¼-inch-thick slices
>
> 4 fresh jalapeño chiles or 6 large serrano chiles (about 2 oz. *total*), halved and seeded
>
> 1 small onion, thinly sliced
>
> ½ cup cider vinegar
>
> 2 dry bay leaves
>
> ½ teaspoon *each* dry oregano and dry thyme
>
> 4 whole black peppercorns, crushed

1. In a wide frying pan, combine garlic and 2 tablespoons water. Cook over medium-high heat, stirring often, until garlic is fragrant and just tinged with brown (3 to 4 minutes). Remove garlic from pan and set aside.

2. Add carrots, chiles, onion, and ¼ cup water to pan. Cook, stirring often, until onion is soft and liquid has evaporated (about 5 minutes).

3. Return garlic to pan; then add ½ cup water, vinegar, bay leaves, oregano, thyme, and peppercorns. Bring to a boil; then reduce heat, cover, and simmer until carrots and chiles are just tender to bite (about 7 minutes).

4. Transfer vegetables and cooking liquid to a nonmetal bowl and let cool to room temperature. Cover and refrigerate until next day; then serve. Or, to store, put pickles in a 3-cup jar, pressing down to fill jar compactly; cover with liquid. Apply lid to jar and refrigerate for up to 1 week. Makes about 3 cups.

Per ¼ cup: 16 calories (3% calories from fat), 0.4 g protein, 4 g carbohydrates, 0.1 g total fat (0 g saturated fat), 0 mg cholesterol, 7 mg sodium

Pictured on facing page

Melon & Cucumber Salad-Salsa

Preparation time: *About 15 minutes*

This mouthwatering blend of melon, papaya, and cool cucumber is delicious with fish, grilled meats, or tamale pie.

> 3 small cantaloupes (about 4 lbs. *total*)
>
> 1 medium-size firm-ripe papaya (about 1 lb.), peeled, seeded, and diced
>
> 1 medium-size cucumber (about 8 oz.), peeled, seeded, and diced
>
> About 2 tablespoons minced fresh mint or 1 teaspoon dry mint, or to taste
>
> 3 tablespoons lime juice
>
> 1 tablespoon honey
>
> Mint sprigs

1. Cut 2 of the melons in half lengthwise. Scoop out and discard seeds. If any of the melon halves does not sit steadily, cut a very thin slice from base so melon sits steadily. Set melon halves aside.

2. Peel, seed, and dice remaining melon. Transfer to a large nonmetal bowl. Add papaya, cucumber, minced mint, lime juice, and honey. Mix gently.

3. Set one melon half in each of 4 bowls (or on each of 4 dinner plates). Spoon a fourth of the fruit mixture into each melon half. If made ahead, cover and refrigerate for up to 4 hours. Just before serving, garnish each melon half with mint sprigs. Makes 4 servings.

Per serving: 135 calories (5% calories from fat), 3 g protein, 33 g carbohydrates, 1 g total fat (0 g saturated fat), 0 mg cholesterol, 28 mg sodium

Nectarine, Plum & Basil Salad-Salsa

Preparation time: About 15 minutes

Sweet, juicy nectarines and plums, diced and tossed with fresh basil, make a lovely summer side dish that's a cross between a fruit salad and a salsa. Be sure the fruit you use is ripe and ready to eat. You can ripen firm-ripe nectarines at room temperature, uncovered, out of direct sun; plums ripen best when grouped inside a loosely closed paper bag. Check fruit daily and refrigerate it, unwashed and packaged airtight, once it's ripe.

- 2 large firm-ripe nectarines (about 12 oz. *total*), pitted and diced
- 2 large firm-ripe plums (about 6 oz. *total*), pitted and diced
- ¼ cup firmly packed fresh basil leaves (minced) or about 1 tablespoon dry basil, or to taste
- 1½ tablespoons red wine vinegar
- 1 tablespoon honey
- 4 to 8 large butter lettuce leaves, rinsed and crisped

1. In a large nonmetal bowl, mix nectarines, plums, basil, vinegar, and honey. If made ahead, cover and refrigerate for up to 4 hours.

2. To serve, place 1 or 2 lettuce leaves on each of 4 dinner plates. Spoon a fourth of the fruit mixture onto each plate. Makes 4 servings.

Per serving: 83 calories (7% calories from fat), 2 g protein, 20 g carbohydrates, 0.7 g total fat (0 g saturated fat), 0 mg cholesterol, 2 mg sodium

Pictured on page 2

Red & Yellow Pepper Salad-Salsa

Preparation time: About 15 minutes

Show off the season's best bell peppers in this nutritious salad. You use the peppers as edible individual bowls—so for the prettiest salad, choose bright, glossy peppers that are firm and well shaped.

- 5 large yellow bell peppers (about 2½ lbs. *total*)
- 1 large red bell pepper (about 8 oz.), seeded and diced
- ⅔ cup peeled, minced jicama
- 2 tablespoons minced cilantro
- 1½ tablespoons distilled white vinegar
- 1 teaspoon honey
  About ⅛ teaspoon ground red pepper (cayenne), or to taste

1. Set 4 of the yellow bell peppers upright, then cut off the top quarter of each. Remove and discard seeds from pepper shells; set shells aside. Cut out and discard stems from top pieces of peppers; then dice these pieces and transfer to a large nonmetal bowl.

2. Seed and dice remaining yellow bell pepper and add to bowl. Then add red bell pepper, jicama, cilantro, vinegar, honey, and ground red pepper; mix gently.

3. Spoon pepper mixture equally into pepper shells. If made ahead, cover and refrigerate for up to 4 hours. Makes 4 servings.

Per serving: 90 calories (5% calories from fat), 3 g protein, 22 g carbohydrates, 0.6 g total fat (0.1 g saturated fat), 0 mg cholesterol, 7 mg sodium

Cucumber & Green Onion Salad

Preparation time: *About 10 minutes*

Marinating time: *20 to 30 minutes*

Typical of the fresh salads served alongside spicy dishes in Mexico, this simple combination of sliced cucumbers and green onions offers cool relief on hot days—and provides a pleasing contrast to zesty dishes in any weather.

- 3 **European cucumbers (about 3 lbs.** *total***), thinly sliced**
- 1 **tablespoon salt**
- ½ **cup thinly sliced green onions**
- ⅓ **cup seasoned rice vinegar; or ⅓ cup distilled white vinegar plus 2½ teaspoons sugar**
- 1 **tablespoon sugar**
  Pepper

1. In a bowl, lightly crush cucumbers and salt with your hands. Let stand for 20 to 30 minutes; then turn into a colander, squeeze gently, and let drain. Rinse with cool water, squeeze gently, and drain well again. (At this point, you may cover and refrigerate until next day.)

2. In a nonmetal bowl, mix cucumbers, onions, vinegar, and sugar. Season to taste with pepper. Serve in bowl or transfer with a slotted spoon to a platter. Serve cold or at room temperature. Makes 8 servings.

Per serving: 38 calories (5% calories from fat), 1 g protein, 9 g carbohydrates, 0.2 g total fat (0.1 g saturated fat), 0 mg cholesterol, 337 mg sodium

Tomatillo & Tomato Salad

Preparation time: *About 15 minutes*

Seasoned with lime and cilantro, a potpourri of tiny tomatoes—red, green, and gold—makes a refreshing salad. When buying tomatoes, purchase only those that have not been refrigerated. Keep unripe fruit at room temperature. Once it's fully ripe, refrigerate it (to slow spoilage) and use it within a day or two.

- 3 **pounds (about 10 cups) ripe cherry tomatoes (red, yellow, yellow-green, orange); include some that are ½ inch or less in diameter**
- 10 **medium-size tomatillos (about 10 oz.** *total***), husked, rinsed, and thinly sliced**
- 1 **fresh jalapeño chile, seeded and minced**
- ½ **cup lightly packed cilantro leaves**
- ¼ **cup lime juice**
  Salt and pepper
  Lime wedges

1. Cut any tomatoes larger than ¾ inch in diameter into halves; then place tomatoes in a nonmetal bowl.

2. Add tomatillos, chile, cilantro, and lime juice; mix gently. Season to taste with salt and pepper; serve with lime wedges. Makes 8 to 10 servings.

Per serving: 40 calories (12% calories from fat), 2 g protein, 8 g carbohydrates, 1 g total fat (0.1 g saturated fat), 0 mg cholesterol, 14 mg sodium

Cilantro Slaw

Preparation time: About 15 minutes

Crisp green-and-red cabbage slaw, seasoned with lots of cilantro and tossed with a tart lime dressing, is a perfect companion for pork, lamb, chicken, or seafood.

    8 ounces green cabbage, very finely shredded
      (about 3 cups)
    8 ounces red cabbage, very finely shredded
      (about 3 cups)
    1 cup firmly packed cilantro leaves, minced
    ¼ cup lime juice
    1 tablespoon *each* water and honey
    ½ teaspoon cumin seeds
      Salt and pepper

1. In a large nonmetal bowl, mix green cabbage, red cabbage, cilantro, lime juice, water, honey, and cumin seeds. Season to taste with salt and pepper. If made ahead, cover and refrigerate for up to 4 hours. Makes 6 servings.

Per serving: 34 calories (5% calories from fat), 1 g protein, 8 g carbohydrates, 0.2 g total fat (0 g saturated fat), 0 mg cholesterol, 14 mg sodium

Pictured on facing page

Orange-Onion Salad with Red Chile Dressing

Preparation time: About 20 minutes

A little heat can heighten flavors. Here, red onion rings and a spicy chile dressing enliven a colorful combination of lettuce, oranges, cucumber, tiny shrimp, and avocado.

      Red Chile Dressing (page 41)
    4 quarts (about 1 lb.) rinsed, crisped leaf
      lettuce, torn into bite-size pieces
    ⅓ pound tiny cooked shrimp
    ½ cup thinly sliced red onion
    1 large cucumber (10 to 12 oz.), peeled (if
      desired) and thinly sliced
    3 small oranges (about 1 lb. *total*)
    1 medium-size firm-ripe avocado
    1 tablespoon lemon juice

1. Prepare Red Chile Dressing; set aside.

2. Place lettuce in a large salad bowl or on a rimmed platter. Arrange shrimp, onion, and cucumber on lettuce.

3. With a sharp knife, cut peel and all white membrane from oranges; then cut oranges crosswise into ¼-inch-thick slices and arrange on salad.

4. Pit and peel avocado; thinly slice lengthwise. Coat slices with lemon juice; then arrange on salad. Pour dressing over salad and mix gently. Makes 8 servings.

Per serving: 106 calories (26% calories from fat), 6 g protein, 16 g carbohydrates, 3 g total fat (0.6 g saturated fat), 37 mg cholesterol, 52 mg sodium

Crisp red onion slices, oranges, creamy avocado, and delicate shrimp accent tender leaf lettuce in our Orange-Onion Salad with Red Chile Dressing (recipe on facing page). To accompany the salad, offer a basket of warm, crusty Bolillos, either purchased or homemade (recipe on page 100).

47

Tomato Relish

Preparation time: *About 10 minutes*

Marinating time: *20 minutes*

Perfectly ripe little Roma tomatoes are the stars of this relish; a sweet-tart seeded dressing adds refreshing flavor without unwanted calories. You might serve the relish alongside your favorite pork or poultry dish.

- 8   medium-size firm-ripe pear-shaped (Roma-type) tomatoes (about 1¼ lbs. *total*)
- ½   cup seasoned rice vinegar; or ½ cup distilled white vinegar plus 1 tablespoon sugar
- 2   tablespoons firmly packed brown sugar
- ½   teaspoon *each* coriander seeds, cumin seeds, and mustard seeds
- ⅛   teaspoon ground red pepper (cayenne)

1. In a 3- to 4-quart pan, bring 2 quarts water to a boil over high heat. Drop in tomatoes and cook for 5 seconds; then lift out and let cool. Remove and discard skins. Cut tomatoes into bite-size pieces and place in a deep nonmetal bowl.

2. Pour water out of pan; then add vinegar, sugar, coriander seeds, cumin seeds, mustard seeds, and red pepper. Bring to a boil over high heat; immediately pour over tomatoes in bowl.

3. Let tomatoes stand for 20 minutes, stirring gently about every 5 minutes. Serve warm or at room temperature. If made ahead, cover and refrigerate until next day. Makes about 2 cups.

Per ¼ cup: 40 calories (6% calories from fat), 0.6 g protein, 10 g carbohydrates, 0.3 g total fat (0 g saturated fat), 0 mg cholesterol, 304 mg sodium

Caesar Salad

Preparation time: *About 15 minutes*

Baking time: *10 to 12 minutes*

First served many years ago in a Tijuana restaurant, the original Caesar salad calls for a dressing made from oil and a raw or coddled egg. This light version of the classic dish features a tangy nonfat sour cream dressing instead.

Garlic Croutons (recipe follows)
- ⅔   cup nonfat or reduced-fat sour cream
- 1   or 2 cloves garlic, minced or pressed
- 2   tablespoons lemon juice
- 1   teaspoon Worcestershire (optional)
- 6   to 8 canned anchovy fillets, rinsed, drained, patted dry, and finely chopped
- 8   cups lightly packed bite-size pieces of rinsed, crisped romaine lettuce
  About ¼ cup grated Parmesan cheese

1. Prepare Garlic Croutons; set aside.

2. In a large nonmetal bowl, beat sour cream, garlic, lemon juice, and Worcestershire (if desired) until blended. Stir in anchovies.

3. Add lettuce to bowl with dressing; mix gently but thoroughly to coat with dressing. Spoon salad onto individual plates and add cheese and croutons to taste. Makes 4 to 6 servings.

Garlic Croutons. In a small bowl, combine 1 tablespoon **olive oil**, 1 tablespoon **water,** and 1 clove **garlic,** minced or pressed. Cut 3 ounces (about 3 slices) **French bread** into ¾-inch cubes and spread in a 10- by 15-inch nonstick rimmed baking pan. Brush oil mixture evenly over bread cubes. Bake in a 350° oven until croutons are crisp and golden (10 to 12 minutes). If made ahead, let cool; then store airtight for up to 2 days. Makes about 3 cups.

Per serving of salad: 70 calories (26% calories from fat), 7 g protein, 5 g carbohydrates, 2 g total fat (0.9 g saturated fat), 6 mg cholesterol, 311 mg sodium

SEVICHE
SALADS

Lovely as light entrées or first courses, these piquant salads taste much like classic seafood *seviche*. But there's an important difference. In authentic seviche, uncooked fish is marinated in citrus juice; the acid slowly firms the flesh, giving it an opaque "cooked" appearance.

Our salads, on the other hand, are made with seafood that actually *is* cooked. Brief simmering in a tart liquid gives fish and shellfish the characteristic seviche flavor, at the same time eliminating any worries one might have about eating raw seafood.

SEVICHE WITH RADISHES & PEAS

To make this cool, satisfying salad, you cook lean white fish in rice vinegar and ginger, then stir in tiny peas and crisp radishes.

- ¾ cup *each* unseasoned rice vinegar and water; or 1 cup distilled white vinegar plus ½ cup water
- 2 tablespoons minced crystallized ginger
- ½ teaspoon coriander seeds
- 1 pound skinless, boneless lean, firm-textured fish such as halibut, mahimahi, or swordfish, cut into ½-inch chunks

- 1 cup frozen tiny peas, thawed
- 1 cup sliced red radishes
  Salt and pepper

1. In a wide nonstick frying pan, bring vinegar, water, ginger, and coriander seeds to a boil over high heat. Add fish. Reduce heat, cover, and simmer until fish is just opaque but still moist in thickest part; cut to test (3 to 4 minutes). With a slotted spoon, transfer fish to a bowl.

2. Boil cooking liquid over high heat, uncovered, until reduced to 1 cup; pour over fish. Cover and refrigerate until cool (at least 1½ hours) or for up to 8 hours.

3. Gently mix peas and radish slices with fish. Spoon into 4 or 6 shallow soup bowls; distribute liquid equally among bowls. Season to taste with salt and pepper. Makes 4 main-dish or 6 first-course servings.

Per main-dish serving: 196 calories (14% calories from fat), 26 g protein, 16 g carbohydrates, 3 g total fat (0.4 g saturated fat), 36 mg cholesterol, 137 mg sodium

LIME & CHIPOTLE SCALLOP SEVICHE

Smoky-hot and tart, this scallop "seviche" is flavored with canned chipotle chiles.

- 1 pound sea or bay scallops
- 1 teaspoon olive oil or salad oil
- ½ cup minced shallots
- ½ teaspoon minced canned chipotle chiles in adobo or adobado sauce; or ½ teaspoon crushed red pepper flakes

- ½ cup *each* lime juice, distilled white vinegar, and water
- 8 ounces jicama
- ⅓ cup minced cilantro
  Lime wedges (optional)

1. Rinse and drain scallops. If scallops are more than ½ inch thick, cut in half horizontally to make thinner rounds; set aside.

2. In a wide nonstick frying pan, combine oil, shallots, and chiles; cook over medium heat, stirring, until shallots are soft (about 3 minutes). Stir in lime juice, vinegar, and water; bring to a boil over high heat. Add scallops, arranging them in pan in a single layer. Reduce heat, cover, and simmer until scallops are just opaque but still moist in center; cut to test (about 2 minutes). With a slotted spoon, transfer scallops to a bowl.

3. Boil cooking liquid over high heat, uncovered, until reduced to 1 cup; pour over scallops. Cover and refrigerate until cool (at least 1½ hours) or for up to 8 hours.

4. Meanwhile, peel jicama, rinse, and cut into ¼-inch-thick matchsticks. Gently mix jicama with scallops and spoon into 4 or 6 shallow soup bowls; distribute liquid equally among bowls. Garnish salads with cilantro and, if desired, lime wedges. Makes 4 main-dish or 6 first-course servings.

Per main-dish serving: 159 calories (12% calories from fat), 20 g protein, 15 g carbohydrates, 2 g total fat (0.2 g saturated fat), 38 mg cholesterol, 203 mg sodium

Capture the flavor of the Yucatán when you serve Lamb Chops with Sour Orange Dressing & Hominy (recipe on page 52). Use some of the tangy dressing to marinate the chops; serve the rest to splash over the cooked meat and herb-seasoned hominy. Oregano sprigs make a nice garnish for each plate.

MEAT

POULTRY

SEAFOOD

A glance through this chapter makes it clear—lean meats, poultry, and seafood merit a leading role in your Mexican menus. You'll find slimmed-down classics like spicy Chili Verde and mole-sauced chicken as well as more innovative selections: a juicy lime-seasoned beef roast, grilled turkey rubbed with onion and cilantro, plump shrimp in a margarita-style tequila sauce, and more.

Pictured on page 50

Lamb Chops with Sour Orange Dressing & Hominy

Preparation time: About 10 minutes

Marinating time: At least 30 minutes

Cooking time: About 15 minutes

The tart-sweet orange-juice mixture that flavors these lamb chops is a popular dressing and marinade on the Yucatán peninsula. The authentic recipe calls for sour Seville oranges, but you can use regular orange juice, too; just be sure to sharpen the flavor with lime (as we do here). And to give the dressing its special zing, don't forget to add a light sprinkling of salt just before serving.

    6   tablespoons orange juice
        About 5 tablespoons lime juice
    ⅛   to ¼ teaspoon sugar
    1   clove garlic, minced or pressed
    1   teaspoon minced shallot
    ⅛   teaspoon pepper
    8   lamb rib chops (about 2 lbs. *total*), cut
        1 inch thick
        Herbed Hominy (recipe follows)
    3   tablespoons finely chopped parsley
        Salt

1. In a nonmetal bowl, mix orange juice, 5 tablespoons of the lime juice (or enough to give orange juice a tart flavor), sugar, garlic, shallot, and pepper.

2. Trim and discard fat from lamb chops. Place chops in a large (1-gallon-size) heavy-duty resealable plastic bag or large nonmetal bowl. Pour ¼ cup of the orange dressing over chops; reserve remaining dressing. Seal bag and rotate to coat chops (or turn chops in bowl to coat, then cover airtight). Refrigerate for at least 30 minutes or until next day, turning occasionally.

3. Prepare Herbed Hominy; keep warm.

4. Lift chops from marinade and drain; discard marinade. Place chops on lightly oiled rack of a broiler pan. Broil chops about 6 inches below heat, turning once, until done to your liking; cut to test (8 to 10 minutes for medium-rare).

5. Transfer chops to dinner plates or a platter; spoon hominy alongside chops. Sprinkle with parsley. Offer remaining orange dressing and salt to add to taste. Makes 4 servings.

Herbed Hominy. In a wide nonstick frying pan, combine 3 cans (about 14 oz. *each*) **yellow hominy,** drained; 1 teaspoon **olive oil** or salad oil; 2 teaspoons **water;** and 1 tablespoon chopped **fresh oregano** or 1 teaspoon dry oregano. Cook over medium-high heat, stirring, until hominy is hot (about 5 minutes). Season to taste with **salt** and **pepper.**

Per serving: 424 calories (29% calories from fat), 25 g protein, 49 g carbohydrates, 13 g total fat (4 g saturated fat), 66 mg cholesterol, 735 mg sodium

Carne Asada

Preparation time: About 10 minutes

Marinating time: At least 30 minutes

Cooking time: 10 to 15 minutes

This traditional main dish is superbly simple: you just marinate strips of skirt steak, skewer them with sweet peppers and fresh rosemary sprigs, and grill lightly.

    ⅓   cup dry red wine
    1   tablespoon *each* lime juice and water
    1¼ pounds skirt steaks, trimmed of fat and cut
        into 6 equal pieces
    4   large bell peppers, about 2 lbs. *total* (use a
        combination of green, red, and yellow bell
        peppers, if desired)
    12 rosemary sprigs (*each* about 3 inches long)
    12 warm corn tortillas (page 25)
        Salt and pepper

1. In a large (1-gallon-size) heavy-duty resealable plastic bag or large nonmetal bowl, combine wine, lime juice, and water. Add meat. Seal bag and rotate to coat meat (or turn meat in bowl to coat, then cover airtight). Refrigerate for at least 30 minutes or until next day, turning occasionally.

2. Seed bell peppers and cut each one lengthwise into sixths.

3. Lift meat from marinade and drain; reserve marinade. On each of six 12- to 15-inch-long metal skewers, weave one piece of meat and 4 bell pepper pieces, rippling meat slightly. For each skewer, tuck 2 rosemary sprigs between meat and skewer.

4. Place skewers on a grill 4 to 6 inches above a solid bed of hot coals. Cook, turning often and brushing with marinade, until meat is done to your liking; cut to test (6 to 10 minutes for rare).

5. Slide food off skewers. Thinly slice meat across the grain; serve with peppers and tortillas. Season to taste with salt and pepper. Makes 6 servings.

Per serving: 311 calories (29% calories from fat), 22 g protein, 32 g carbohydrates, 10 g total fat (4 g saturated fat), 47 mg cholesterol, 140 mg sodium

Roast Beef with Rice

Preparation time: About 10 minutes

Roasting time: About 40 minutes

For a Mexican twist on all-American beef roast, baste the meat with a lime-coriander marinade.

- 1¾ **pounds boneless beef triangle tip (tri-tip) or top round roast, trimmed of fat**
- ¼ **cup lime juice**
- ⅓ **cup water**
- 1 **tablespoon reduced-sodium soy sauce**
- ¾ **teaspoon ground coriander**
- 2 **cloves garlic, minced or pressed**
  About 2 cups beef broth
- 1 **cup long-grain white rice**
- ¼ **cup sliced green onions**
  Salt and pepper

1. Set meat in an 8- by 12-inch roasting pan. In a nonmetal bowl, mix lime juice, water, soy sauce, coriander, and garlic. Measure out ⅓ cup of the lime mixture to use for basting; set remainder aside to use in rice. Brush some of the reserved ⅓ cup lime mixture evenly over meat.

2. Roast in a 450° oven, basting 4 times with lime mixture, until a meat thermometer inserted in thickest part of meat registers 135°F for rare (about 40 minutes). After 25 minutes, check temperature every 5 to 10 minutes. If pan drippings begin to burn, add 4 to 6 tablespoons water to pan and stir to scrape browned bits free.

3. While meat is roasting, measure remaining lime mixture; add enough broth to make 2 cups liquid. Pour into a 2- to 3-quart pan; bring to a boil over medium-high heat. Add rice; return to a boil, stirring. Reduce heat, cover, and simmer until liquid has been absorbed and rice is tender to bite (about 20 minutes). Remove from heat; keep warm.

4. When meat is done, transfer it to a board, cover loosely, and let stand for 10 minutes. Then pour drippings from roasting pan into rice; also stir in any meat juices that have accumulated on board. Add onions and stir to blend.

5. To serve, thinly slice meat across the grain; serve with rice. Season to taste with salt and pepper. Makes 6 servings.

Per serving: 291 calories (18% calories from fat), 31 g protein, 27 g carbohydrates, 6 g total fat (2 g saturated fat), 80 mg cholesterol, 461 mg sodium

Pork in Escabeche Sauce

Preparation time: About 15 minutes

Roasting time: 20 to 30 minutes

Escabeche, a piquant blend of spices and garlic, gives roasted pork tenderloin a wonderful flavor.

  Escabeche Paste (recipe follows)
- 2 **pork tenderloins (about 12 oz.** *each***), trimmed of fat and silvery membrane**
  About 4 large oranges (about 3 lbs. *total***), peeled (if desired) and sliced crosswise**

1. Prepare Escabeche Paste; spread evenly over pork tenderloins. (At this point, you may cover and refrigerate until next day.)

2. Place tenderloins, side by side, on a rack in a 9- by 13-inch baking pan. Roast in a 450° oven until a meat thermometer inserted in thickest part of meat registers 155°F (20 to 30 minutes). After 15 minutes, check temperature every 5 to 10 minutes.

3. When meat is done, cover it loosely and let stand for 10 minutes. To serve, thinly slice meat across the grain; transfer to a platter. Surround meat with orange slices. Makes 6 servings.

Escabeche Paste. Mix 4 cloves **garlic,** minced or pressed; 1 tablespoon *each* **orange juice** and **white wine vinegar;** 1 teaspoon **dry oregano;** ¾ teaspoon **ground cinnamon;** ½ teaspoon *each* **ground allspice, ground cloves, ground cumin,** and **ground coriander;** ¼ teaspoon **black pepper;** and ⅛ teaspoon **ground red pepper** (cayenne).

Per serving: 203 calories (13% calories from fat), 26 g protein, 28 g carbohydrates, 3 g total fat (1 g saturated fat), 74 mg cholesterol, 60 mg sodium

Herbed Pork Chops with Apples

Preparation time: About 10 minutes

Cooking time: About 30 minutes

Sweet apple jelly and tart cider vinegar combine in a tempting sauce for quickly cooked pork chops. To complete the dish, poach sliced Golden Delicious apples in the pan juices; then spoon them alongside the meat.

- 6 center-cut loin pork chops (about 2 lbs. *total*), trimmed of fat
  Pepper
- ¼ cup apple jelly
- 1 tablespoon *each* Dijon mustard and water
- ½ teaspoon ground cumin
- 3 large Golden Delicious apples (about 1½ lbs. *total*)
- ¼ cup cider vinegar

1. Sprinkle chops with pepper; then cook in a wide nonstick frying pan over medium-high heat, turning once, until well browned on both sides (about 14 minutes).

2. In a small bowl, mix jelly, mustard, water, and cumin. Spoon evenly over chops. Reduce heat to low, cover, and cook until chops look faintly pink to white in center; cut to test (about 10 minutes; meat should still be moist). With a slotted spoon or a fork, transfer chops to a platter; keep warm.

3. Peel, core, and thinly slice apples. Add apples and vinegar to pan; stir to coat apples with pan juices, scraping browned bits free. Cover and cook over medium heat until apples are barely tender when pierced (about 5 minutes).

4. With a slotted spoon, transfer apples to platter with chops. Offer hot pan juices to pour over chops and apples. Makes 6 servings.

Per serving: 256 calories (27% calories from fat), 23 g protein, 24 g carbohydrates, 8 g total fat (3 g saturated fat), 64 mg cholesterol, 144 mg sodium

Pictured on facing page

Chili Verde

Preparation time: About 15 minutes

Cooking time: About 1½ hours

Chili verde is a classic pork stew that's popular throughout Mexico. We suggest serving it with rice, but it's just as good with warm corn or flour tortillas.

- 1 pound lean boneless pork shoulder, trimmed of fat and cut into ¾-inch cubes
- 1 large can (about 28 oz.) tomatoes
- 2 medium-size onions, chopped
- 1½ cups thinly sliced celery
- 1 teaspoon dry oregano
- ½ teaspoon rubbed sage
- 2 dry bay leaves
- 1 large green bell pepper (about 8 oz.), seeded and chopped
- 2 medium-size fresh green Anaheim, poblano, or other large mild chiles (about 4 oz. *total*), seeded and chopped
  About 4 cups hot cooked rice
  Cilantro sprigs

1. Place pork in a wide nonstick frying pan or 3- to 4-quart pan. Drain about ½ cup liquid from tomatoes into pan. Cover and bring to a boil over high heat; then reduce heat and simmer for 30 minutes.

2. Uncover pan; add onions, celery, oregano, and sage. Cook over high heat, stirring often, until liquid has evaporated and pan drippings are richly browned (8 to 10 minutes). Add bay leaves. Stir in tomatoes and their remaining liquid (break tomatoes up with a spoon); stir to scrape browned bits free. Reduce heat, cover, and simmer for 30 more minutes. Stir in bell pepper and chiles; cover and continue to simmer, stirring occasionally, until meat is very tender when pierced (about 15 more minutes). If chili is too thin, uncover and simmer until it's as thick as you like.

3. To serve, spoon chili over rice and garnish with cilantro sprigs. Makes 4 servings.

Per serving: 538 calories (17% calories from fat), 31 g protein, 79 g carbohydrates, 10 g total fat (3 g saturated fat), 76 mg cholesterol, 469 mg sodium

Filled with succulent chunks of pork, Chili Verde (recipe on facing page)
owes its rich flavor to slow, gentle simmering. Serve the spicy stew over rice
for a satisfying meal. Round out the menu with ripe tropical fruits
and glasses of iced tea.

FILLINGS

To add interest to tacos, burritos, chimichangas, tostadas, or enchiladas, simply experiment with different fillings. You'll find five choices on these pages—two made with poultry, one with beef, and two with beans. For other ideas, take a look through the preceding and following chapters. Tinga (page 24) is great in enchiladas; the bean-and-corn fajita filling on page 17 is delicious in tacos, too.

Though some of these fillings get more than 30 percent of their calories from fat, they still have a place in a lowfat diet; just combine them with vegetables, tortillas, and other lowfat ingredients, as we do throughout this book. For suggested uses for each filling, see the recipe introductions below.

SHREDDED CHICKEN FILLING

Shredded chicken breast cloaked in a rich sauce of chiles, tomatoes, and onions makes a moist, versatile fill-

ing. Try it in Chicken Chimichangas (page 22) or as an alternative to Tinga in Shredded Beef Tostadas (page 24).

- 6 dried ancho or pasilla chiles (about 1½ oz. *total*)
- 1 teaspoon salad oil
- 2 large onions, chopped
- 2 cloves garlic, minced or pressed
- 1 can (about 14½ oz.) tomatoes
- 2 teaspoons sugar
- 1 teaspoon dry oregano
- ½ teaspoon ground cumin
- 2 cups finely shredded cooked chicken or turkey breast
  Salt and pepper

1. Place chiles on a baking sheet and toast in a 300° oven until fragrant (3 to 4 minutes). Remove from oven; let cool. Discard stems, seeds, and veins; then place chiles in a bowl, cover with 1½ cups boiling water, and let stand until pliable (about 30 minutes).

2. While chiles are soaking, place oil, onions, garlic, and 1 tablespoon water in a wide nonstick frying pan. Cook over medium heat, stirring often, until mixture is deep golden (20 to 30 minutes); if onions stick to pan or pan appears dry, add more water, 1 tablespoon at a time.

3. Drain chiles, discarding liquid. In a blender or food processor, whirl chiles, tomatoes and their liquid, sugar, oregano, and cumin until smoothly puréed.

4. Stir chicken and chile-tomato mixture into onion mixture. Reduce heat and simmer, uncovered, stirring occasionally, until mixture is thick and flavors are blended (about 10 minutes). Season to taste with salt and pepper. Makes about 3 cups.

TURKEY CHORIZO SAUSAGE

Traditional chorizo is based on pork, but to make a leaner version of this spicy sausage, we've used ground turkey breast. Our chorizo is wonderful with scrambled eggs and, of course, in Turkey Chorizo Enchiladas (page 20).

- 1 large onion, chopped
- 2 teaspoons *each* chili powder and dry oregano
- 1 teaspoon *each* cumin seeds and crushed red pepper flakes
- 1 cup low-sodium chicken broth
- 1 pound ground turkey or chicken breast
- ½ cup cider vinegar

1. In a wide frying pan, combine onion, chili powder, oregano, cumin seeds, red pepper flakes, and broth. Bring to a boil over high heat; boil, stirring occasionally, until liquid has evaporated and browned bits stick to pan. Add 2 tablespoons water, stirring to scrape browned bits free; cook until mixture begins to brown again. Repeat this deglazing step, adding 2 tablespoons of water each time, until onion is a rich brown color.

2. Add 2 tablespoons more water, then crumble turkey into pan; cook, stirring, until browned bits stick to pan. Repeat deglazing step, adding vinegar in 2-tablespoon portions, until mixture is a rich brown color. If made ahead, let cool; then cover and refrigerate until next day. Makes about 3½ cups.

BIRRIA-STYLE BRISKET

The central Mexican state of Zacatecas is well known for a savory stew called *birria*. Because sheep ranching is common in the region, the stew is traditionally based on lamb—but today, you'll find beef birria as well. Our version of the dish features a fresh brisket, slowly oven-braised with mild chiles, vinegar, and onions. Torn into shreds, the tender meat makes a great filling for burritos or Shredded Beef Tostadas (page 24).

- 4 dried red New Mexico or California chiles (1 to 1½ oz. *total*); or ¼ cup chili powder
- 2 small dried hot red chiles
- 4 cups water
- 1½ cups dry red wine
- ¼ cup red wine vinegar
- 6 cloves garlic, peeled
- 1½ teaspoons *each* ground cumin and dry oregano
- ½ teaspoon ground cinnamon
- 1 piece center-cut beef brisket (2½ to 3 lbs.), trimmed of fat
- 4 large onions, thinly sliced

1. Remove and discard stems, seeds, and veins from New Mexico and hot chiles. Rinse chiles, place in a 2- to 3-quart pan, and add water. Bring to a boil over high heat. Remove from heat, cover, and let stand until pliable (about 30 minutes). Drain chiles; then place chiles (or chili powder) in a blender or food processor and add wine, vinegar, garlic, cumin, oregano, and cinnamon. Whirl until smoothly puréed.

2. Place brisket in a 12- by 15-inch roasting pan; top with chili purée and onions. Cover pan tightly with foil. (At this point, you may refrigerate until next day.)

3. Bake, covered, in a 350° oven until meat is very tender when

pierced (about 4 hours). Let meat cool slightly, then shred with 2 forks; stir to mix with onions and pan juices. If made ahead, cover and refrigerate for up to 2 days. To reheat, bake, covered, in a 350° oven until heated through (about 45 minutes). Makes about 9 cups.

REFRIED BLACK BEANS

There are many versions of this long-time favorite, but the basic ingredients remain the same: beans, onions, and a hint of smoky bacon (which we use here) or lard. Serve the beans as a side dish; or use them to make Black Bean & Fresh Corn Nachos (page 12).

- 4 ounces bacon, coarsely chopped
- 2 medium-size onions, chopped
- 2 cloves garlic, minced or pressed
- 2 cans (about 15 oz. *each*) black beans; or 4 cups cooked (about 2 cups dried) black beans
  About 2 tablespoons distilled white vinegar, or to taste
  Pepper

1. In a wide nonstick frying pan, cook bacon over medium heat, stirring often, until it begins to brown and drippings form in pan (about 4 minutes). Discard all but 1 tablespoon of the drippings.

2. Add onions and garlic to pan; cook, stirring often, until onions are soft and bacon is browned (about 7 minutes).

3. Drain beans, reserving ½ cup of the liquid from cans.

4. Add beans, reserved liquid (use ½ cup low-sodium chicken broth if using home-cooked beans), and vinegar to pan. Coarsely mash beans with a spoon. Season to taste with pepper. Heat until steaming. If made ahead, let cool; then cover and refrigerate until next day. Reheat before serving. Makes about 3¼ cups.

ZESTY REFRIED BEANS

These mashed and "fried" beans are just right at any meal, from breakfast to supper; try them in Egg & Bean Burritos, page 86. Caramelized onions and a touch of cider vinegar add flavor without fat.

- 2 medium-size onions, chopped
- 2 cloves garlic, minced or pressed
- 2 teaspoons salad oil
- 2 cans (about 15 oz. *each*) pinto or other beans; or 4 cups cooked (about 2 cups dried) pinto or other beans
- 2 tablespoons cider vinegar
  About ⅛ teaspoon ground red pepper (cayenne), or to taste
  Salt (optional)

1. In a wide nonstick frying pan, combine onions, garlic, oil, and 1 tablespoon water. Cook over medium heat, stirring often, until mixture is deep golden (20 to 30 minutes); if onions stick to pan bottom or pan appears dry, add more water, 1 tablespoon at a time.

2. Drain beans, reserving ½ cup of the liquid from cans.

3. To pan, add beans, reserved liquid (use ½ cup low-sodium chicken broth if using home-cooked beans), vinegar, and red pepper. Coarsely mash beans with a spoon. Season to taste with salt, if desired. Heat until steaming. If made ahead, let cool; then cover and refrigerate until next day. Reheat before serving. Makes about 3¼ cups.

Chicken breasts topped with Mexico's famous mole sauce are perfect for a special dinner. Serve Jalapeño Chicken with Mole Poblano (recipe on facing page) with beer, warm tortillas, and other side dishes of your choice. You might garnish each plate with lime wedges and shiny fresh chiles.

Pictured on facing page

Jalapeño Chicken with Mole Poblano

Preparation time: About 25 minutes

Cooking time: About 20 minutes

The single word *mole* names a whole category of Mexican sauces. One popular member of the group is mellow, slightly sweet *mole poblano*, well known for its inclusion of bitter chocolate. Traditional moles are made with chiles, fruits, nuts, spices, thickeners, and—often—volumes of lard. Our streamlined mole poblano eliminates much of the fat and replaces the chocolate with unsweetened cocoa, yet its flavor is still as deliciously complex as that of the original.

To accompany the chicken and sauce, you might serve warm corn tortillas (page 25), hot cooked rice, and Zesty Refried Beans (page 57) sprinkled with *cotija* (a Mexican cheese) or grated Parmesan. For dessert, offer a fresh fruit plate.

- 1 **tablespoon sesame seeds**
- 1 **large onion, chopped**
- 4 **cloves garlic, minced or pressed**
- 1 **small very ripe banana, chopped**
- ¼ **cup chopped pitted prunes**
- 2 **tablespoons raisins**
- 1 **tablespoon creamy peanut butter**
- 5 **tablespoons unsweetened cocoa powder**
- 3 **tablespoons chili powder**
- 2 **teaspoons sugar**
- ½ **teaspoon ground cinnamon**
- ⅛ **teaspoon *each* ground coriander, ground cumin, ground cloves, and anise seeds, crushed**
- 2 **cups low-sodium chicken broth**
- 1 **small can (about 6 oz.) tomato paste**
- 8 **skinless, boneless chicken breast halves (about 6 oz. *each*)**
- 2 **tablespoons mild jalapeño jelly, melted; or 2 tablespoons apple jelly, melted and mixed with ⅟₁₆ teaspoon ground red pepper (cayenne)**
  Salt
  Lime wedges

1. Toast sesame seeds in a wide nonstick frying pan over medium heat until golden (about 4 minutes), stirring often. Transfer to a bowl; set aside.

2. To pan, add onion, garlic, banana, prunes, raisins, peanut butter, and 3 tablespoons water. Cook over medium heat, stirring often, until mixture is richly browned (10 to 15 minutes); if pan appears dry, add more water, 1 tablespoon at a time. Stir in cocoa, chili powder, sugar, cinnamon, coriander, cumin, cloves, anise seeds, and ¾ cup of the broth. Bring mixture to a boil over medium-high heat.

3. Transfer hot onion mixture to a food processor or blender and add tomato paste, 2 teaspoons of the sesame seeds, and a little of the remaining broth. Whirl until smoothly puréed; then stir in remaining broth. Cover and keep warm. Or, if made ahead, let cool; then cover and refrigerate for up to 3 days (freeze for longer storage). Reheat before continuing.

4. While onion mixture is browning, rinse chicken and pat dry. Place jelly in a bowl and stir to soften; add chicken and mix to coat. Then place chicken in a lightly oiled 10- by 15-inch rimmed baking pan. Bake in a 450° oven until meat in thickest part is no longer pink; cut to test (12 to 15 minutes).

5. To serve, spoon some of the warm mole sauce onto dinner plates; top with chicken, then more mole sauce. Sprinkle with remaining 1 teaspoon sesame seeds. Season to taste with salt; serve with lime wedges. Makes 8 servings.

Per serving: 267 calories (18% calories from fat), 33 g protein, 23 g carbohydrates, 6 g total fat (1 g saturated fat), 74 mg cholesterol, 305 mg sodium

Arroz con Pollo

Preparation time: About 15 minutes

Cooking time: About 1 hour and 10 minutes

This classic chicken-and-rice dish is perfect for a casual Mexican-style dinner.

- 1 can (about 14½ oz.) tomatoes
  About 1½ cups low-sodium chicken broth
- 1 chicken (3 to 3½ lbs.), cut up and skinned
- 1 teaspoon salad oil
- 1 large onion, chopped
- 1 small green pepper (about ⅓ lb.), seeded and chopped
- 2 cloves garlic, minced or pressed (optional)
- 1 cup long-grain white rice
- 1 teaspoon dry oregano
- ¼ teaspoon *each* ground cumin and pepper
- 1 dry bay leaf
- 1 package (about 10 oz.) frozen tiny peas, thawed
  Salt
- ¼ cup thinly sliced green onions

1. Drain liquid from tomatoes into a glass measure; add enough broth to make 2 cups liquid.

2. Rinse chicken and pat dry. Heat oil in a 4- to 5-quart pan over medium-high heat. Add several pieces of chicken (do not crowd pan) and 2 tablespoons water; cook, turning as needed, until chicken is browned on all sides (about 10 minutes). Add more water, 1 tablespoon at a time, if pan appears dry. Repeat to brown remaining chicken, setting pieces aside as they are browned. Discard all but 1 teaspoon of the drippings.

3. Add chopped onion, bell pepper, and garlic (if desired) to pan; cook, stirring, until onion is soft (about 5 minutes). Stir in tomatoes (break them up with a spoon), broth mixture, rice, oregano, cumin, pepper, and bay leaf. Bring to a boil.

4. Return chicken to pan. Reduce heat, cover, and simmer until meat near thighbone is no longer pink; cut to test (about 45 minutes). Add more broth as needed to prevent sticking. Stir in peas; season to taste with salt. Just before serving, garnish with green onions. Makes 6 servings.

Per serving: 332 calories (15% calories from fat), 32 g protein, 38 g carbohydrates, 5 g total fat (1 g saturated fat), 83 mg cholesterol, 283 mg sodium

Chili & Anise Chicken Tortas

Preparation time: About 15 minutes

Cooking time: 15 to 20 minutes

Succulent chicken, steeped in a spicy-sweet broth, makes a lively-tasting filling for French rolls or fresh *semitas*.

- 1 pound skinless, boneless chicken thighs
- 4 cups water
- 2 cups low-sodium chicken broth
- ¼ cup *each* chili powder and firmly packed brown sugar
- 2 teaspoons dry oregano
- 1 teaspoon anise seeds
  About 1 tablespoon red wine vinegar, or to taste
- 2 tablespoons *each* chopped cilantro and thinly sliced green onion
- 4 French rolls (*each* about 6 inches long) or Semitas (page 100)
- 8 to 12 butter lettuce leaves, rinsed and crisped
  Condiments: Pickled Vegetables (page 43), avocado slices, and asadero or string cheese

1. Rinse chicken and pat dry; set aside. In a 4- to 5-quart pan with a tight-fitting lid, combine water, broth, chili powder, sugar, oregano, and anise seeds. Bring to a rolling boil over high heat. Remove pan from heat and immediately add chicken. Cover pan and let stand until meat in thickest part is no longer pink; cut to test (15 to 20 minutes; *do not uncover* until ready to test). If chicken is not done, return it to hot water, cover, and let steep for 2 to 3 more minutes.

2. Drain chicken, reserving 2 cups of the cooking liquid. Return reserved liquid to pan. Bring to a boil over high heat; boil until reduced to ½ cup, watching closely to prevent scorching.

3. Serve chicken and sauce warm or cold. To serve, stir vinegar, cilantro, and onion into sauce. Cut chicken across the grain into thin slanting slices; set aside. Cut rolls in half lengthwise and moisten cut surfaces evenly with sauce. Fill rolls with chicken and lettuce. Offer additional sauce and condiments to add to taste. Makes 4 servings.

Per serving: 472 calories (13% calories from fat), 32 g protein, 69 g carbohydrates, 7 g total fat (1 g saturated fat), 94 mg cholesterol, 1,804 mg sodium

Picadillo Stew

Preparation time: About 15 minutes

Cooking time: 20 to 25 minutes

Its name comes from the word *picar* ("to mince")—and as you might expect, *picadillo* is made with chopped ingredients. This version of the dish is a hearty turkey stew, richly seasoned with raisins, spices, and almonds. To complete the meal, serve Blue Corn Muffins (page 104) alongside.

- 2 tablespoons slivered almonds
- ¼ cup dry red wine
- 2 tablespoons reduced-sodium soy sauce
- 1 tablespoon lemon juice
- 2 teaspoons sugar
- 1 teaspoon *each* ground cumin, ground coriander, and chili powder
- ⅛ teaspoon ground cinnamon
- 4 teaspoons cornstarch
- 1 teaspoon salad oil
- 1 pound boneless turkey breast, cut into 1-inch chunks
- 1 large onion, chopped
- 2 cloves garlic, minced or pressed
- 1 can (about 14½ oz.) tomatoes
- ⅔ cup raisins
  Pepper

1. Toast almonds in a small frying pan over medium heat until golden (5 to 7 minutes), stirring often. Transfer almonds to a bowl and set aside.

2. In a small bowl, mix wine, soy sauce, lemon juice, sugar, cumin, coriander, chili powder, cinnamon, and cornstarch until smooth. Set aside.

3. Heat oil in a wide nonstick frying pan or 5-quart pan over high heat. Add turkey, onion, and garlic. Cook, stirring, until meat is no longer pink in thickest part; cut to test (10 to 15 minutes). Add water, 1 tablespoon at a time, if pan appears dry. Add tomatoes and their liquid (break tomatoes up with a spoon), wine mixture, and raisins to pan. Bring to a boil; boil, stirring, just until thickened.

4. To serve, ladle stew into bowls and sprinkle with almonds. Season to taste with pepper. Makes 4 servings.

Per serving: 317 calories (14% calories from fat), 32 g protein, 36 g carbohydrates, 5 g total fat (1 g saturated fat), 70 mg cholesterol, 538 mg sodium

Onion-Cilantro Turkey

Preparation time: About 15 minutes

Marinating time (optional): 2 to 3 hours

Cooking time: 7 to 9 minutes

A pungent seasoning rub of garlic, cilantro, ginger, and lime makes these grilled turkey tenderloins especially flavorful. To increase the meat's succulence, "cure" it for a few hours with a mixture of salt and sugar.

Salt Cure (optional; recipe follows)
- 1½ pounds turkey breast tenderloins
  Onion Mixture (recipe follows)
  Cilantro sprigs
  Whole green onions, ends trimmed
  Lime wedges

1. Prepare Salt Cure, if desired. Rinse turkey and pat dry. If desired, rub Salt Cure over turkey; place in a bowl, cover, and refrigerate for 2 to 3 hours. Then rinse turkey well with cool water and pat dry.

2. If turkey pieces are large, cut into serving-size portions. Place each piece of turkey between 2 sheets of plastic wrap; pound meat gently and evenly with a flat-surfaced mallet until about ½ inch thick. (At this point, you may cover and refrigerate until next day.)

3. Prepare Onion Mixture and rub over turkey pieces. Place turkey on a lightly greased grill 4 to 6 inches above a solid bed of hot coals. Cook, turning as needed to brown evenly, until meat in thickest part is no longer pink; cut to test (7 to 9 minutes).

4. To serve, garnish turkey with cilantro sprigs and onions. Serve with lime wedges. Makes 6 servings.

Salt Cure. Mix 1 tablespoon **salt** and 1½ teaspoons **sugar.**

Onion Mixture. In a small bowl, mix ¼ cup thinly sliced **green onions;** 2 tablespoons minced **cilantro;** 3 cloves **garlic,** pressed or minced; 1 tablespoon minced **fresh ginger;** and 1 teaspoon *each* **coarsely ground pepper** and grated **lime peel.**

Per serving (without Salt Cure): 131 calories (5% calories from fat), 28 g protein, 1 g carbohydrates, 1 g total fat (0.2 g saturated fat), 70 mg cholesterol, 57 mg sodium

Pictured on facing page

Whitefish with Soft Cornmeal

Preparation time: About 10 minutes

Cooking time: About 20 minutes

Cornmeal, one of Mexico's staple foods, is prepared like Italian polenta in this recipe: it's cooked in broth until tender and creamy. Top the chile- and cumin-seasoned cornmeal with baked white fish fillets.

> 4⅓ cups low-sodium chicken broth
> 1 cup yellow cornmeal or polenta
> ½ teaspoon cumin seeds
> 1 small can (about 4 oz.) diced green chiles
> 1 pound skinless, boneless sea bass, orange roughy, or sole fillets, divided into 4 equal pieces
> 1 small red bell pepper (about ⅓ lb.), seeded and minced
> 1 tablespoon cilantro leaves
> Salt
> Lemon slices

1. In a 3- to 4-quart pan, stir together broth, cornmeal, and cumin seeds until smoothly blended. Bring to a boil over high heat, stirring often with a long-handled wooden spoon (mixture will spatter). Reduce heat and simmer gently, uncovered, stirring often, until cornmeal tastes creamy (about 20 minutes). Stir in chiles.

2. When cornmeal is almost done, rinse fish, pat dry, and arrange in a single layer in a 9- by 13-inch baking pan. Bake in a 475° oven until fish is just opaque but still moist in thickest part; cut to test (about 6 minutes).

3. To serve, spoon soft cornmeal equally onto 4 dinner plates. Top each serving with a piece of fish; sprinkle with bell pepper and cilantro. Season to taste with salt and serve with lemon slices. Makes 4 servings.

Per serving: 285 calories (15% calories from fat), 27 g protein, 32 g carbohydrates, 5 g total fat (1 g saturated fat), 47 mg cholesterol, 310 mg sodium

Salmon & Squash with Brown Sugar & Lime

Preparation time: About 10 minutes

Baking time: About 1¼ hours

The combination of lime and brown sugar is popular in Mexican cooking; in this easy one-pan meal, the sweet-tart flavors enhance baked salmon and winter squash. (*Piloncillo* is unrefined sugar shaped into hard cones; if you can't find it, regular brown sugar will do.)

> 2 pounds banana or Hubbard squash, cut into 4 equal pieces
> 1½ cups low-sodium chicken broth
> 4 baby salmon fillets (about 5 oz. *each*)
> ½ teaspoon salad oil
> 1 cone piloncillo (about 3 oz.), finely chopped; or ¼ cup firmly packed brown sugar
> ¼ cup lime juice
> Lime wedges
> Salt and pepper

1. Scoop out and discard any seeds from squash. Lay squash, skin side up, in a 10- by 15-inch or 11- by 14-inch rimmed baking pan; pour in broth. Bake in a 350° oven until squash is tender when pierced (about 1 hour). Remove from oven; increase oven temperature to 450°.

2. Rinse fish and pat dry. Turn squash over and push to one end of pan. Lift opposite end of pan so that any liquid runs down to mix with squash; then spread oil over exposed pan bottom. Place fish fillets side by side (they can overlap slightly) in oiled part of pan. Mix piloncillo and lime juice; spoon about half the mixture over fish and squash.

3. Return pan to oven and bake until fish is just opaque but still moist in thickest part; cut to test (about 8 minutes). After fish has baked for 5 minutes, spoon remaining lime mixture over fish and squash.

4. To serve, transfer fish and squash to four dinner plates; garnish with lime wedges. Stir pan juices to blend, then pour into a small pitcher. Season fish and squash to taste with pan juices, salt, and pepper. Makes 4 servings.

Per serving: 331 calories (29% calories from fat), 32 g protein, 28 g carbohydrates, 11 g total fat (2 g saturated fat), 78 mg cholesterol, 100 mg sodium

*Here's an unusual combination that's sure to please: colorful Whitefish with
Soft Cornmeal (recipe on facing page). Just bake lean sea bass fillets, then
arrange them atop yellow cornmeal simmered to creaminess in a cumin-
seasoned broth. Sprinkle minced red pepper and cilantro over all.*

63

Whole Tilapia with Onion & Lemon

Preparation time: About 15 minutes

Baking time: 20 to 25 minutes

Farmed in both Mexico and the United States, tilapia is a perchlike fish with a clean, delicate flavor similar to that of petrale sole. It's appealingly lean, but remains moist and tender after cooking. For an intimate dinner for two, try baking a whole dressed tilapia on a bed of ginger-spiked onion and lemon slices.

- 1¼ **pounds red onions, cut into ⅛-inch-thick slices**
- 3 **tablespoons lemon juice**
- 1 **tablespoon minced fresh ginger**
- 1 **whole tilapia (about 1½ lbs.), dressed (gutted, with head and tail attached)**
- 1 **tablespoon extra-virgin olive oil**
- 2 **large lemons**
- 3 **tablespoons minced cilantro**
  Salt and pepper

1. In a large bowl, mix onions, lemon juice, and ginger. Reserve 1 or 2 onion slices; arrange remaining slices over bottom of a 9- by 13-inch or shallow 4- to 5-quart baking dish.

2. Rinse fish and pat dry. Brush both sides of fish with oil; then place fish on top of onion mixture.

3. Cut a ½-inch slice from each end of each lemon; stuff fish cavity with lemon ends, reserved onion slices, and half the cilantro. Thinly slice remaining piece of each lemon; tuck slices around fish. Sprinkle remaining cilantro over onion and lemon in baking dish. Bake in a 400° oven until a meat thermometer inserted in thickest part of fish registers 135°F and flesh is just opaque but still moist; cut to test (20 to 25 minutes).

4. To serve, gently pull skin from fish; then spoon fish, onions, and lemon slices onto 2 dinner plates. Season to taste with salt and pepper. Makes 2 servings.

Per serving: 359 calories (22% calories from fat), 38 g protein, 40 g carbohydrates, 10 g total fat (2 g saturated fat), 82 mg cholesterol, 177 mg sodium

Snapper Veracruz

Preparation time: About 10 minutes

Cooking time: 20 to 25 minutes

Named after the beautiful seacoast town where it originated, this snapper specialty features fresh fillets topped with a cinnamon-spiced sauce of bell pepper, tomatoes, and olives.

- 1 **teaspoon salad oil or olive oil**
- 1 **small green or red bell pepper (about ⅓ lb.), seeded and chopped**
- 1 **large onion, chopped**
- 3 **cloves garlic, minced or pressed (optional)**
- 2 **tablespoons water**
- 1 **small can (about 4 oz.) diced green chiles**
- ¼ **cup sliced pimento-stuffed green olives**
- 3 **tablespoons lime juice**
- 1 **teaspoon ground cinnamon**
- ¼ **teaspoon white pepper**
- 1 **can (about 14½ oz.) stewed tomatoes**
- 4 **snapper or rockfish fillets (about 2 lbs. *total*)**
- 1 **tablespoon drained capers**

1. Heat oil in a wide nonstick frying pan over medium-high heat. Add bell pepper, onion, garlic (if desired), and water; cook, stirring often, until vegetables are tender-crisp to bite (3 to 5 minutes).

2. Add chiles, olives, lime juice, cinnamon, and white pepper; cook for 1 more minute. Add tomatoes to pan (break tomatoes up with a spoon, if needed); then bring mixture to a boil. Boil, stirring often, until sauce is slightly thickened (about 5 minutes).

3. Rinse fish, pat dry, and arrange in a lightly greased 9- by 13-inch baking dish. Pour sauce over fish. Bake in a 350° oven until fish is just opaque but still moist in thickest part; cut to test (10 to 15 minutes).

4. With a slotted spoon, transfer fish and sauce to four dinner plates. Sprinkle with capers. Makes 4 servings.

Per serving: 310 calories (16% calories from fat), 49 g protein, 16 g carbohydrates, 6 g total fat (1 g saturated fat), 84 mg cholesterol, 842 mg sodium

Pictured on back cover

Margarita Shrimp

Preparation time: About 15 minutes

Cooking time: About 10 minutes

For an elegant, easy-to-fix main course, stir-fry shrimp in tequila and lime, then serve over thinly sliced red onions. Quick cooking keeps the shellfish tender and succulent.

- ¼ **cup gold or white tequila**
- ½ **teaspoon grated lime peel**
- 2 **tablespoons *each* lime juice and water**
- 2 **tablespoons minced cilantro or parsley**
- 1 **tablespoon honey**
- ⅛ **teaspoon white pepper**
- 1 **pound large shrimp (about 25 per lb.), shelled and deveined**
  About 2 teaspoons orange-flavored liqueur, or to taste (optional)
- 2 **large red onions**
  Salt
  Cilantro sprigs
  Lime wedges

1. In a nonmetal bowl, mix tequila, lime peel, lime juice, water, minced cilantro, honey, and white pepper.

2. Pour tequila mixture into a wide nonstick frying pan. Add shrimp and cook over medium-high heat, stirring, until shrimp are just opaque but still moist in center; cut to test (3 to 4 minutes). With a slotted spoon, transfer shrimp to a bowl and keep warm. Bring cooking liquid to a boil over high heat; boil until reduced to ⅓ cup. Remove pan from heat; stir in liqueur, if desired.

3. While cooking liquid is boiling, thinly slice onions. Arrange onion slices in a single layer on a rimmed platter. To serve, spoon shrimp and cooking liquid over onion slices. Season to taste with salt; garnish with cilantro sprigs and lime wedges. Makes 4 servings.

Per serving: 173 calories (9% calories from fat), 21 g protein, 19 g carbohydrates, 2 g total fat (0.3 g saturated fat), 140 mg cholesterol, 153 mg sodium

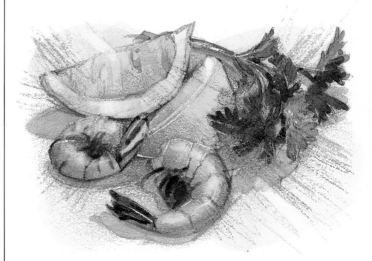

Garlic Shrimp with Rice

Preparation time: About 10 minutes

Cooking time: About 5 minutes

Shrimp are plentiful along the Mexican coast. In this fragrant dish, the plump shellfish are infused with garlic and a touch of butter.

- 2 **teaspoons butter or margarine**
- 2 **teaspoons olive oil**
- 3 **cloves garlic, minced or pressed**
- 3 **tablespoons water**
- 1 **pound large shrimp (about 25 per lb.), shelled and deveined**
  About 4 cups hot cooked rice
- 3 **tablespoons chopped parsley**
  Salt and pepper
  Lemon wedges

1. Melt butter in a wide nonstick frying pan over medium-high heat. Add oil, garlic, water, and shrimp. Cook, stirring, until shrimp are just opaque but still moist in center; cut to test (3 to 4 minutes).

2. To serve, spoon rice onto a platter or four dinner plates; spoon shrimp and pan juices over rice. Sprinkle with parsley. Season to taste with salt and pepper, then serve with lemon wedges. Makes 4 servings.

Per serving: 403 calories (15% calories from fat), 24 g protein, 59 g carbohydrates, 6 g total fat (2 g saturated fat), 145 mg cholesterol, 161 mg sodium

Elegant as a first course, Artichokes with Shrimp & Cilantro Salsa
(recipe on page 68) are also an impressive light entrée. Try serving them with
sparkling mineral water and a selection of rolls from a Mexican market.

VEGETABLES

BEANS

RICE

Bright vegetables, savory legumes, and whole grains bring nutrition and diversity to Mexican meals. To add interest to any entrée, just serve Cocoa-glazed Carrots & Onions, Cerveza Beans, or Lemon-Caper Rice alongside. Some of these recipes work well as main dishes: Chayote with Turkey, for example, makes a delicious lunch or dinner.

Pictured on page 66

Artichokes with Shrimp & Cilantro Salsa

Preparation time: About 25 minutes

Cooking time: About 35 minutes

Big artichoke halves filled with a spicy shrimp-cilantro "salsa" make an attractive first course. Pickled scallions, available in well-stocked supermarkets and Asian markets, add a sweet crunch to the salsa.

- ½ **cup seasoned rice vinegar; or ½ cup distilled white vinegar plus 1 tablespoon sugar**
- 1 **tablespoon mustard seeds**
- 1 **teaspoon whole black peppercorns**
- 4 **thin quarter-size slices fresh ginger**
- 3 **large artichokes (about 12 oz. *each*), *each* 4 to 4½ inches in diameter**
- 12 **ounces tiny cooked shrimp**
- ⅓ **cup minced pickled scallions**
- ¼ **cup minced cilantro**
- ¼ **cup minced fresh mint or 1 tablespoon dry mint**
- 2 **tablespoons reduced-sodium soy sauce**
- ¼ **to ½ teaspoon chili oil**
  Mint or cilantro sprigs

1. In a 6- to 8-quart pan, combine ¼ cup of the vinegar, mustard seeds, peppercorns, ginger, and 4 quarts water. Cover and bring to a boil over high heat.

2. Meanwhile, remove coarse outer leaves from artichokes and trim stems flush with bases. With a sharp knife, cut off top third of each artichoke. With scissors, trim thorny tips from remaining leaves. Immerse artichokes in cold water and swish back and forth vigorously to release debris; then lift artichokes from water and shake briskly to drain.

3. Lower artichokes into boiling vinegar-water mixture. Then reduce heat and simmer, covered, until artichoke bottoms are tender when pierced (about 35 minutes). Drain, reserving cooking liquid. Let artichokes stand until they are cool enough to handle.

4. Pour artichoke cooking liquid through a fine strainer set over a bowl; discard ginger and

reserve mustard seeds and peppercorns. Place shrimp in strainer. Rinse shrimp with cool water; then drain well, place in a bowl, and mix with reserved seasonings, remaining ¼ cup vinegar, scallions, minced cilantro, minced mint, soy sauce, and chili oil. (At this point, you may cover and refrigerate artichokes and shrimp mixture separately until next day.)

5. With a long, sharp knife, cut each artichoke in half lengthwise. Remove sharp-pointed inner leaves and scoop out fuzzy centers. Set each artichoke half on a salad plate. Spoon shrimp mixture equally into artichokes; garnish with mint sprigs. Makes 6 servings.

Per serving: 122 calories (11% calories from fat), 15 g protein, 13 g carbohydrates, 2 g total fat (0.2 g saturated fat), 111 mg cholesterol, 911 mg sodium

Cocoa-glazed Carrots & Onions

Preparation time: About 15 minutes

Cooking time: 20 to 30 minutes

In Mexico, chocolate isn't just for desserts—it's used in savory dishes, too. Here, a small amount of unsweetened cocoa brings mellow, complex flavor to a sauce for baby carrots and pearl onions.

- 10 **ounces fresh pearl onions (*each* about 1 inch in diameter); or 1 package (about 10 oz.) frozen pearl onions**
- 1½ **pounds baby or small carrots, peeled**
- 1 **tablespoon butter or margarine**
- 2 **tablespoons lemon juice**
- 1 **tablespoon *each* water, honey, and unsweetened cocoa powder**
- 1 **teaspoon grated fresh ginger**

1. If using fresh onions, place them in a bowl and cover with boiling water. Let stand for 2 to 3 minutes. Drain; then pull or slip off skins and discard them. Also trim root and stem ends of onions.

2. Place peeled fresh onions or frozen onions in a wide nonstick frying pan. Barely cover with water and bring to a boil over high heat. Reduce heat, cover, and simmer gently until onions are tender when pierced (10 to 15 minutes). Drain onions, pour out of pan, and set aside.

3. If using baby carrots, leave whole; if using small carrots, cut diagonally into ¼-inch-thick slices. Place carrots in pan used for onions, barely cover with water, and bring to a boil over high heat. Reduce heat, cover, and simmer gently until carrots are just tender when pierced (7 to 10 minutes). Drain carrots and set aside.

4. In pan, combine butter, lemon juice, the 1 tablespoon water, honey, cocoa, and ginger. Stir over medium-high heat until smoothly blended. Add carrots and onions. Stir gently over high heat until sauce is thick enough to cling to vegetables (2 to 3 minutes). Makes 6 servings.

Per serving: 92 calories (21% calories from fat), 2 g protein, 18 g carbohydrates, 2 g total fat (1 g saturated fat), 5 mg cholesterol, 61 mg sodium

Roasted Potatoes & Carrots with Citrus Dressing

Preparation time: About 15 minutes

Baking time: 35 to 45 minutes

Roasting does wonderful things for vegetables. Carrots taste intensely sweet; potatoes take on a mellower flavor. Here, the richly browned vegetables are tossed with a light citrus-chile dressing for a zesty Mexican touch. Serve the colorful combination with any main dish.

> **Citrus Dressing (page 41)**
> 2 **pounds small red thin-skinned potatoes (*each* about 1½ inches in diameter), scrubbed and cut into 1-inch chunks**
> 4 **teaspoons olive oil or salad oil**
> 4 **medium-size carrots (about 1 lb. *total*), cut into 1-inch chunks**
> **Salt and pepper**
> **Basil sprigs**

1. Prepare Citrus Dressing; refrigerate.

2. In a lightly oiled 10- by 15-inch rimmed baking pan, mix potatoes with 2 teaspoons of the oil. In another lightly oiled 10- by 15-inch rimmed baking pan, mix carrots with remaining 2 teaspoons oil. Bake potatoes and carrots in a 475° oven, stirring occasionally, until richly browned (35 to 45 minutes); switch positions of baking pans halfway through baking.

3. In a shallow bowl, combine potatoes, carrots, and Citrus Dressing. Serve hot or warm. Before serving, season to taste with salt and pepper; garnish with basil sprigs. Makes 6 to 8 servings.

Per serving: 177 calories (15% calories from fat), 3 g protein, 35 g carbohydrates, 3 g total fat (0.4 g saturated fat), 0 mg cholesterol, 74 mg sodium

Orange & Rum Sweet Potatoes

Preparation time: About 10 minutes

Cooking time: About 20 minutes

Simmered sweet potato slices in an orange-rum sauce make an easy, interesting side dish that's especially tasty with roast pork or chicken.

> 1 **teaspoon salad oil**
> 3 **medium-size sweet potatoes (about 1¼ lbs. *total*), peeled and cut into ¼-inch-thick slices**
> ¾ **cup low-sodium chicken broth**
> ½ **cup orange juice**
> 1 **tablespoon rum**
> **About 2 teaspoons honey, or to taste**
> 2 **teaspoons cornstarch**
> ⅛ **teaspoon white pepper**
> **Salt**
> 1 **tablespoon minced parsley**

1. Heat oil in a wide nonstick frying pan over medium-high heat. Add potatoes and ½ cup of the broth. Bring to a boil over medium-high heat; then reduce heat, cover, and simmer until potatoes are tender when pierced (about 10 minutes). Uncover and continue to cook, stirring occasionally, until liquid has evaporated and potatoes are tinged with brown (about 5 more minutes).

2. In a bowl, mix remaining ¼ cup broth, orange juice, rum, honey, cornstarch, and white pepper. Add cornstarch mixture to pan and bring to a boil over medium heat; boil, stirring, just until thickened. Season to taste with salt and sprinkle with parsley. Makes 4 servings.

Per serving: 157 calories (10% calories from fat), 2 g protein, 32 g carbohydrates, 2 g total fat (0.3 g saturated fat), 0 mg cholesterol, 24 mg sodium

Pictured on facing page

White Bean & Tomato Salad

Preparation time: *About 15 minutes*

Cooking time: *About 1 hour and 10 minutes*

Delicious as an accompaniment, this savory salad of warm white beans and roasted tomatoes is just as good as a lunch or supper main course.

- 1 **large red onion, cut into ¾-inch chunks**
- 2½ **teaspoons olive oil**
- 2 **tablespoons balsamic or red wine vinegar**
- 12 **to 14 medium-size firm-ripe pear-shaped (Roma-type) tomatoes (1¾ to 2 lbs. *total*), cut lengthwise into halves**
  Salt
- 3 **cans (about 15 oz. *each*) cannellini (white kidney beans)**
- 2 **tablespoons *each* chopped fresh thyme and chopped fresh basil; or 2 teaspoons *each* dry thyme and dry basil**
  Pepper

1. In a lightly oiled 8- to 10-inch-square baking pan, mix onion, ½ teaspoon of the oil, and vinegar. Arrange tomatoes, cut side up, in a lightly oiled 9- by 13-inch baking pan; rub with remaining 2 teaspoons oil, then sprinkle with salt.

2. Bake onion and tomatoes in a 475° oven until edges of onion chunks and tomato halves are dark brown (40 to 50 minutes for onion, about 1 hour and 10 minutes for tomatoes); switch positions of baking pans halfway through baking.

3. Pour beans and their liquid into a 2- to 3-quart pan. Add fresh thyme (or both dry thyme and dry basil). Bring to a boil; reduce heat and simmer for 3 minutes, stirring. Pour beans into a fine strainer set over a bowl; reserve liquid. Place beans in a serving bowl; tap herbs from strainer into beans.

4. Chop 8 tomato halves; stir into beans along with fresh basil (if used) and onion. Add some of the reserved liquid to moisten, if desired. Season to taste with salt and pepper. Arrange remaining 16 to 20 tomato halves around edge of salad. Makes 8 side-dish or 4 main-dish servings.

Per side-dish serving: 179 calories (11% calories from fat), 10 g protein, 32 g carbohydrates, 2 g total fat (0.3 g saturated fat), 0 mg cholesterol, 566 mg sodium

Chayote with Turkey

Preparation time: *About 15 minutes*

Cooking time: *About 1½ hours*

Mild-flavored chayote—a green, pear-shaped summer squash—is delicious when stuffed and baked. Try these turkey-filled chayote halves as a hearty side dish or light entrée.

- 3 **chayotes (about 12 oz. *each*)**
- 1 **pound ground turkey**
- 1 **medium-size onion, minced**
- 4 **cloves garlic, minced or pressed**
- ½ **teaspoon *each* ground allspice and coarsely ground pepper**
- ⅛ **teaspoon ground cloves**
- ⅓ **cup raisins**
- 1 **can (about 6 oz.) tomato paste**
- 2 **tablespoons dry red wine**
  Reduced-fat sour cream (optional)

1. In a 4- to 5-quart pan, bring 2 quarts water to a boil over high heat. Add chayotes; reduce heat, cover, and simmer until chayotes are tender when pierced (about 40 minutes). Drain and let cool. Cut chayotes in half lengthwise and scoop out pulp, leaving ½-inch-thick shells. Chop pulp.

2. Crumble turkey into a wide nonstick frying pan. Add ¼ cup water, onion, garlic, allspice, pepper, and cloves. Cook over medium-high heat, stirring, until browned bits stick to pan. Add ¼ cup more water, stirring to scrape browned bits free; cook until mixture begins to brown again. Repeat this deglazing step, adding 2 to 3 tablespoons of water each time, until mixture is a rich brown color (about 20 minutes *total*). Stir in chayote pulp, raisins, tomato paste, and wine.

3. Spoon filling equally into chayote halves. Place halves, filled side up, in a 9- by 13-inch baking dish. Cover tightly and bake in a 350° oven until filling is hot in center (about 25 minutes). Top with sour cream, if desired. Makes 6 servings.

Per serving: 214 calories (27% calories from fat), 17 g protein, 24 g carbohydrates, 7 g total fat (2 g saturated fat), 55 mg cholesterol, 305 mg sodium

For a protein-packed side dish that's easy on the cook, choose warm White Bean & Tomato Salad (recipe on facing page). To pick up the salad's herb flavors, garnish the dish with fresh basil and thyme sprigs. Cool Chile-Mint Lemonade (recipe on page 112) is just right for sipping alongside.

HOW TO COOK LEGUMES

Visit any Mexican market and you'll find dried legumes in variety, from pinto and black beans to Great Northerns and tiny lentils. These foods play an important role in Mexico's cooking. They offer great nutrition—lots of protein, little fat, and no cholesterol—and their varied flavors allow for endless seasonings and culinary combinations.

The recipes in this book call for only a few kinds of legumes, but you should feel free to experiment with other choices. On this page, we provide a guide for cooking some of the most widely available types. If you'd like to substitute home-cooked beans for canned ones, keep in mind that a 15-ounce can holds about 2 cups cooked (about 1 cup dried) beans.

To ensure good texture and digestibility, always prepare legumes properly. Rinse them in a colander; as you rinse, remove and discard any debris and imperfect legumes. Drain. Then soak (if necessary) and cook as directed at right. If you wish to add salt, do so *after* cooking; otherwise, the legumes may become tough.

Soaking legumes. All legumes except black-eyed peas, lentils, and split peas should be soaked. Use the quick-soak method if you're in a hurry; otherwise, soak overnight.

Quick soaking. For each pound of dried legumes, bring 2 quarts water to a boil in a 4- to 5-quart pan over high heat. Add rinsed legumes; boil for 10 minutes. Remove from heat, cover, and let stand for 1 hour. Drain, discarding water; rinse well.

Overnight soaking. For each pound of dried legumes, pour 2 quarts of water into a large bowl. Add rinsed legumes; let soak at room temperature until next day. Drain, discarding water; rinse well.

Cooking legumes. Cooking times vary depending on the type of legume and the length of time it has been stored. The older the legume, the longer it takes to cook—so don't combine newly purchased legumes with those already on your shelf.

For each pound of dried legumes (unsoaked weight), pour 2 quarts cold water into a 3- to 4-quart pan. Add legumes (soaked, if necessary) and bring to a boil over high heat. Then reduce heat, cover, and simmer until tender to bite (see our times; or follow package directions). If needed, add water to keep legumes moist. Start tasting when the minimum recommended time is up; when they're done, legumes should be tender but not mushy.

Black beans (turtle beans). Popular in Latin American and Caribbean cuisine, black beans have a rich, mellow flavor. Soak first. Cook for 1½ to 2 hours.

Black-eyed peas. Beige ovals with distinctive black spots, black-eyed peas have an earthy taste. Do not soak. Cook for about 50 minutes.

Garbanzo beans (chick peas, ceci beans). Rich, nutty flavor and toothsome texture make garbanzos a natural for soups and salads. Soak first. Cook for 2 to 2½ hours.

Great Northern beans. These mild-flavored, medium-size white beans are similar in shape to kidney beans. You can use them in place of cannellini (white kidney beans). Soak first. Cook for 1 to 1½ hours.

Kidney beans. Kidney beans have a firm texture and a meaty flavor. The red variety is more widely sold than the white type; if you can't find the white beans (cannellini), substitute Great Northerns. Soak first. Cook for 1 to 1½ hours.

Lentils. Mild and earthy in flavor, disk-shaped lentils come in many varieties, including brown, green, and pink types. Decorticated (skinless) lentils turn mushy if overcooked. Do not soak. Cook for about 40 minutes.

Lima beans. Limas cook up softer than other legumes. Serve as a side dish or in casseroles and soups. Soak first. Cook for about 1 hour.

Pinto, pink, red, cranberry, and other speckled beans. These beans may be mottled or solid in color; all work well in chilis, casseroles, and soups. Soak first. Cook for about 1½ hours.

Split peas. These green or yellow halved peas have a distinctive flavor and a soft texture; use them in soups and side dishes. Do not soak. Cook for 35 to 45 minutes.

White navy beans. Small, creamy white navy beans are the classic choice for baked beans. Soak first. Cook for about 1 hour.

Cerveza Beans

Preparation time: About 5 minutes

Cooking time: About 20 minutes

Spicy-sweet beans flavored with a hint of beer are just right with your favorite meat or poultry entrées; you might try them with Shredded Beef Tostadas (page 24) or Oven-baked Turkey Fajitas (page 17).

> 4 slices bacon, coarsely chopped
> 1 large onion, chopped
> 2 cans (about 15 oz. *each*) pinto beans; or 4 cups cooked (about 2 cups dried) pinto beans
> 1 can (about 8 oz.) tomato sauce
> ½ cup regular or nonalcoholic beer, or to taste
> 3 tablespoons molasses
> 1½ teaspoons *each* dry mustard and Worcestershire
> ¼ teaspoon pepper
>   Salt

1. In a 3- to 4-quart pan, cook bacon and onion over medium heat, stirring often, until browned bits form on pan bottom and onion is soft (8 to 10 minutes). Discard any fat.

2. Drain beans, reserving ¼ cup of the liquid from cans. To pan, add beans and reserved liquid (if using home-cooked beans, use ¼ cup low-sodium chicken broth mixed with ½ teaspoon cornstarch). Then stir in tomato sauce, ¼ cup of the beer, molasses, mustard, Worcestershire, and pepper. Bring to a boil; then reduce heat so beans boil gently. Cook, stirring occasionally, until flavors are blended—about 10 minutes. (At this point, you may let cool, then cover and refrigerate for up to 2 days; reheat before continuing.)

3. To serve, stir in remaining ¼ cup beer and season to taste with salt. Makes 4 to 6 servings.

Per serving: 219 calories (14% calories from fat), 10 g protein, 37 g carbohydrates, 4 g total fat (1 g saturated fat), 4 mg cholesterol, 867 mg sodium

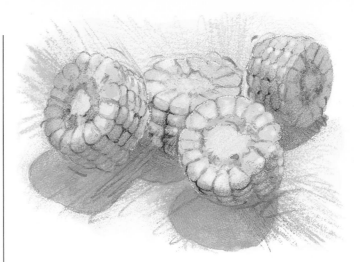

Seasoned Sweet Corn

Preparation time: About 10 minutes

Cooking time: About 5 minutes

Fresh corn flavored with a tart marinade has the natural goodness so typical of Mexican food. Easily assembled in just a few minutes, the dish is both nutritious and flavorful.

> 6 medium-size ears corn (about 3 lbs. *total*), *each* about 8 inches long, husks and silk removed
>   Vinegar Marinade (recipe follows)
>   Salt and pepper

1. With a sharp, heavy knife, cut corn crosswise into 1-inch rounds. In a large pan, bring 4 quarts water to a boil over high heat. Add corn, cover, and cook until hot (3 to 4 minutes). Drain corn well and pour into a shallow rimmed dish (about 9 by 13 inches).

2. Prepare Vinegar Marinade. Pour marinade over corn; let stand, frequently spooning marinade over corn, until corn is cool enough to eat out of hand. Season to taste with salt and pepper. Makes 6 servings.

Vinegar Marinade. In a small pan, combine ½ cup **distilled white vinegar;** ¼ cup **lime juice;** 1 cup minced **onion;** 3 tablespoons **sugar;** 1 small jar (about 2 oz.) **diced pimentos;** 1 teaspoon **mustard seeds;** and ¼ to ½ teaspoon **crushed red pepper flakes.** Bring to a boil over high heat; then boil, stirring, just until sugar is dissolved. Use hot.

Per serving: 115 calories (9% calories from fat), 3 g protein, 27 g carbohydrates, 1 g total fat (0.1 g saturated fat), 0 mg cholesterol, 17 mg sodium

*A flour tortilla "lid" covers hot Pueblo Stew (recipe on facing page),
a colorful combination of beans, summer squash, hominy, and tomatoes.
Embellish each serving with mild jack cheese, sour cream, and,
if you like, grilled green onions.*

Pictured on facing page

Pueblo Stew

Preparation time: 20 to 30 minutes

Cooking time: About 45 minutes

Garlic and chili powder add a little spice to this mellow vegetable stew. Serve it with warm, soft flour tortillas; if you like, present the tortillas as "lids" for individual bowls of stew.

- 1 teaspoon olive oil or salad oil
- 1 large onion, chopped
- 2 cloves garlic, minced or pressed
- 1½ tablespoons chili powder
- 2 teaspoons cumin seeds
- 1 teaspoon dry oregano
- 1 *each* medium-size zucchini, pattypan, and crookneck squash (about 6 oz. *each*), cut into 1-inch chunks
- 1 can (about 14 oz.) yellow hominy, drained
- 1 pound firm-ripe tomatoes, chopped
- 4 ounces green beans, cut into 1-inch lengths
- 2 cans (about 15 oz. *each*) pinto beans, drained and rinsed; or 4 cups cooked (about 2 cups dried) pinto beans, drained and rinsed
- 4 vegetable or chicken bouillon cubes
- 2 cups water
- 1 tablespoon minced cilantro
- 4 warm flour tortillas (page 25)
   Cilantro sprigs
   Reduced-fat sour cream (optional)
   Shredded jack cheese (optional)

1. Heat oil in a 4- to 5-quart pan over medium-high heat. Add onion, garlic, chili powder, cumin seeds, and oregano. Cook, stirring often, until onion begins to brown (about 8 minutes); add water, 1 tablespoon at a time, if pan appears dry. Stir in squash, hominy, and tomatoes; cook until tomatoes begin to fall apart (about 5 minutes).

2. Stir in green beans, pinto beans, bouillon cubes, and 2 cups water; bring to a boil. Then reduce heat and simmer, uncovered, stirring occasionally, until green beans and squash are tender when pierced and mixture has the consistency of a thick stew (about 30 minutes). If mixture is too thick, add a little water; if it's too thin, continue to simmer, uncovered, until it's as thick as you like.

3. To serve, stir in minced cilantro; then ladle stew into 4 straight-sided 2-cup bowls. Lay a warm tortilla over each bowl; if desired, tie tortilla in place with raffia or string. Garnish with cilantro sprigs. Eat tortillas with stew; add sour cream and cheese to taste, if desired. Makes 4 servings.

Per serving: 411 calories (15% calories from fat), 17 g protein, 73 g carbohydrates, 7 g total fat (1 g saturated fat), 0 mg cholesterol, 1,686 mg sodium

All-vegetable Chili

Preparation time: About 15 minutes

Cooking time: About 30 minutes

It's every bit as hearty as traditional chili—but this sturdy dish is made entirely without meat. Try it with Cornhusk Muffins (page 93) alongside.

- 2 medium-size carrots (about 8 oz. *total*), chopped
- 1 large onion, coarsely chopped
- ¼ cup water
- 1 can (about 14½ oz.) tomatoes
- 1 can (about 15 oz.) pinto beans; or 2 cups cooked (about 1 cup dried) pinto beans
- 1 can (about 15 oz.) red kidney beans; or 2 cups cooked (about 1 cup dried) red kidney beans
- 2 tablespoons chili powder
   About ½ cup plain nonfat yogurt
   Salt and crushed red pepper flakes

1. In a 4- to 5-quart pan, combine carrots, onion, and water. Cook over high heat, stirring often, until liquid has evaporated and vegetables begin to brown and stick to pan (about 10 minutes).

2. Add tomatoes and their liquid to pan; break tomatoes up with a spoon. Stir in all beans and their liquid (if using home-cooked beans, add 1 cup low-sodium chicken broth mixed with 1 teaspoon cornstarch). Add chili powder; stir to scrape browned bits free. Bring to a boil; then reduce heat and simmer, uncovered, until flavors are blended (about 15 minutes). If chili is too thick, add a little water; if it's too thin, continue to simmer until it's as thick as you like.

3. Ladle chili into bowls. Add yogurt, salt, and red pepper flakes to taste. Makes 4 servings.

Per serving: 261 calories (6% calories from fat), 15 g protein, 50 g carbohydrates, 2 g total fat (0.2 g saturated fat), 1 mg cholesterol, 1,057 mg sodium

Black Bean & Jicama Salad

Preparation time: About 15 minutes

Refreshing and easy to prepare, this salad is good with simple entrées such as Red Pepper Flan (page 88) or Pork in Escabeche Sauce (page 53).

- 1 can (about 15 oz.) black beans, drained and rinsed; or 2 cups cooked (about 1 cup dried) black beans, drained and rinsed
- 1 cup peeled, finely chopped jicama
- ¼ cup crumbled panela or feta cheese
- 3 tablespoons lime juice
- ⅓ cup minced cilantro
- 2 tablespoons thinly sliced green onion
- 2 teaspoons honey
- ¼ teaspoon crushed red pepper flakes
- 4 to 8 butter lettuce leaves, rinsed and crisped

1. In a bowl, combine beans, jicama, cheese, lime juice, cilantro, onion, honey, and red pepper flakes. Mix well. If made ahead, cover and refrigerate for up to 4 hours.

2. To serve, spoon bean mixture into lettuce leaves. Makes 4 servings.

Per serving: 164 calories (13% calories from fat), 10 g protein, 28 g carbohydrates, 2 g total fat (1 g saturated fat), 8 mg cholesterol, 100 mg sodium

Roasted Pepper & Black Bean Salad

Preparation time: About 15 minutes

Cooking time: About 8 minutes

Authentic Mexican ingredients, carefully chosen for their contrasting textures and flavors, distinguish this cold bean dish. You combine nutty-tasting black beans with roasted red peppers, cilantro, and a little onion, then enliven the mixture with a tart-sweet vinegar dressing.

- Roasted Red Bell Peppers (directions follow)
- ½ cup seasoned rice vinegar; or ½ cup distilled white vinegar plus 1 tablespoon sugar
- 1 tablespoon *each* water, olive oil, and honey
- ½ teaspoon chili oil
- 3 cans (about 15 oz. *each*) black beans, drained and rinsed; or 6 cups cooked (about 3 cups dried) black beans, drained and rinsed
- ¼ cup minced cilantro
- 2 tablespoons thinly sliced green onion
- Salt
- Cilantro sprigs

1. Prepare Roasted Red Bell Peppers; set aside.

2. In a bowl, mix vinegar, water, olive oil, honey, and chili oil. Add beans and roasted peppers; mix gently but thoroughly. (At this point, you may cover and refrigerate until next day.)

3. To serve, stir minced cilantro and onion into bean mixture. Season to taste with salt and garnish with cilantro sprigs. Makes 6 servings.

Roasted Red Bell Peppers. Cut 2 large **red bell peppers** (about 1 lb. *total*) in half lengthwise. Set pepper halves, cut side down, in a 10- by 15-inch rimmed baking pan. Broil 4 to 6 inches below heat until charred all over (about 8 minutes). Cover with foil and let cool in pan. Then remove and discard skins, stems, and seeds; cut peppers into strips or chunks.

Per serving: 295 calories (11% calories from fat), 16 g protein, 52 g carbohydrates, 4 g total fat (1 g saturated fat), 0 mg cholesterol, 400 mg sodium

Roasted Garlic & Broccoli

Preparation time: About 15 minutes

Cooking time: About 20 minutes

For a lovely complement to Onion-Cilantro Turkey (page 61) or Carne Asada (page 52), serve this combination of tender-crisp broccoli and sweet roasted garlic in a light sesame dressing.

- 3 **large heads garlic (about 12 oz.** *total***)**
- 2 **teaspoons olive oil**
  About 1¼ pounds (about 9 cups) broccoli flowerets
- 2 **tablespoons reduced-sodium soy sauce**
- 1 **teaspoon Oriental sesame oil**

1. Separate garlic heads into cloves; then peel cloves and place in a lightly oiled 8- to 10-inch-square baking pan. Mix in olive oil. Bake in a 475° oven just until garlic is tinged with brown; do not scorch (about 20 minutes; remove smaller cloves as they brown, if needed). Set aside.

2. While garlic is roasting, in a 5- to 6-quart pan, bring 3 to 4 quarts water to a boil over high heat. Add broccoli and cook until tender-crisp to bite (about 5 minutes). Drain, immerse in ice water until cool, and drain again.

3. In a shallow bowl, mix soy sauce and sesame oil. Add garlic cloves and broccoli; toss gently to mix. Makes 6 servings.

Per serving: 123 calories (18% calories from fat), 6 g protein, 22 g carbohydrates, 3 g total fat (0.3 g saturated fat), 0 mg cholesterol, 229 mg sodium

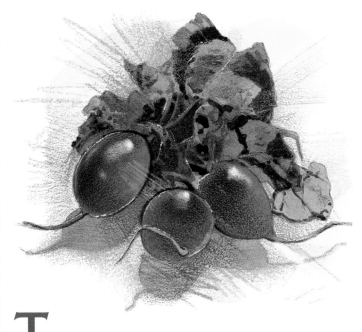

Triple Corn Stew

Preparation time: About 5 minutes

Cooking time: 25 to 30 minutes

Spicy chorizo seasons a hearty stew featuring corn in three forms: hominy, creamed corn, and the whole kernels. Top each bowlful with a peppery garnish of crisp radish slices.

- 8 **ounces chorizo sausages, casings removed**
- 1 **can (about 14 oz.) yellow hominy, drained**
- 1 **can (about 17 oz.) cream-style corn**
- 2 **cups fresh-cut yellow or white corn kernels (from 2 large ears corn); or 1 package (about 10 oz.) frozen corn kernels, thawed; or 1 can (about 1 lb.) corn kernels, drained**
- 1 **teaspoon cornstarch**
- ½ **cup low-sodium chicken broth**
  Thinly sliced red radishes

1. Coarsely chop or crumble sausage; place in a 4- to 5-quart pan. Cook over medium heat, stirring, until well browned (15 to 20 minutes). Discard fat.

2. Add hominy, cream-style corn, and corn kernels to pan. Cook, stirring occasionally, until heated through (about 5 minutes).

3. In a small bowl, mix cornstarch and broth; stir into corn mixture and cook, stirring, until stew comes to a boil. Ladle stew into wide bowls; garnish with radishes. Makes 4 servings.

Per serving: 347 calories (27% calories from fat), 14 g protein, 54 g carbohydrates, 11 g total fat (3 g saturated fat), 32 mg cholesterol, 744 mg sodium

Couscous Paella

Preparation time: About 15 minutes

Cooking time: 20 to 25 minutes

Brought to Mexico by the Spanish conquistadores, paella is traditionally based on rice. Here, though, it's made with quick-cooking couscous—semolina flour formed into tiny grains. Studded with sausage, shrimp, and bell pepper, the dish is bound to become a favorite one-pan entrée.

- 4 ounces chorizo sausages, casings removed
- 1 large onion
- 1 bottle (about 8 oz.) clam juice
- 1¼ cups low-sodium chicken broth
- 2 teaspoons cumin seeds
- 1½ cups couscous
- 1 medium-size red bell pepper (about 6 oz.), seeded and chopped
- 8 ounces tiny cooked shrimp
  Lime or lemon wedges

1. Crumble chorizo into a wide nonstick frying pan; then add onion. Cook over medium heat, stirring often, until well browned (15 to 20 minutes); add water, 1 tablespoon at a time, if pan appears dry. Add clam juice, broth, and cumin seeds. Bring to a rolling boil over medium-high heat; then stir in couscous.

2. Cover pan and remove from heat. Let stand until liquid has been absorbed (about 5 minutes). Stir in bell pepper and top with shrimp. Serve with lime wedges. Makes 4 to 6 servings.

Per serving: 384 calories (25% calories from fat), 21 g protein, 49 g carbohydrates, 11 g total fat (4 g saturated fat), 104 mg cholesterol, 378 mg sodium

Pictured on facing page

Fruited Quinoa Salad

Preparation time: About 15 minutes

Cooking time: About 30 minutes

Quinoa, often called the "super grain" thanks to its high protein content, is the base for this simple yet elegant salad. You'll find quinoa in well-stocked supermarkets and natural-foods stores; be sure to rinse it before cooking to remove the slightly bitter coating.

- 2 tablespoons pine nuts or slivered almonds
- 1¼ cups (about 10 oz.) dried apricots
- 1½ cups quinoa or 1 cup bulgur
- 2 teaspoons olive oil or salad oil
- 2 or 3 cups low-sodium chicken broth
- 2 teaspoons grated lemon peel
- 2 tablespoons lemon juice
- 1 cup dried currants
  Salt

1. Toast pine nuts in a small frying pan over medium heat until golden brown (3 to 5 minutes), stirring often. Transfer nuts to a bowl; set aside. Coarsely chop ½ cup of the apricots; set aside.

2. Place quinoa in a fine strainer; rinse thoroughly with water (bulgur needs no rinsing). Heat oil in a 3- to 4-quart pan over medium heat. Add quinoa or bulgur; cook, stirring often, until grain turns a slightly darker brown (8 to 10 minutes).

3. To pan, add broth (3 cups for quinoa, 2 cups for bulgur), lemon peel, and lemon juice. Bring to a boil over high heat. Reduce heat, cover, and simmer until grain is just tender to bite (10 to 15 minutes). Drain and discard any liquid from grain. Stir chopped apricots and ½ cup of the currants into grain. Let stand until warm; or let cool, then cover and refrigerate until next day.

4. To serve, season quinoa mixture to taste with salt. Mound mixture in center of a serving dish or large rimmed platter. Garnish with remaining ¾ cup apricots, remaining ½ cup currants, and pine nuts. Makes 6 servings.

Per serving: 352 calories (15% calories from fat), 10 g protein, 70 g carbohydrates, 6 g total fat (0.9 g saturated fat), 0 mg cholesterol, 55 mg sodium

If you're not familiar with quinoa, here's a great way to get acquainted with this high-protein grain: Fruited Quinoa Salad (recipe on facing page). Dressed up with apricots, currants, and toasted pine nuts, the lemon-scented side dish is especially good with roast chicken.

Bulgur Relish

Preparation time: About 15 minutes

Cooking time: About 30 minutes

Serve this vegetable-dotted "relish" as you would salsa, as an accent for meats, poultry, or fish. It's based on chewy bulgur; carrots, zucchini, and red bell pepper add bright color and fresh flavor.

- 2 teaspoons olive oil or salad oil
- 2 medium-size carrots (about 8 oz. *total*), shredded
- 2 medium-size zucchini (about 12 oz. *total*), shredded
- 1 medium-size red or green bell pepper (about 6 oz.), seeded and slivered
- 3 cloves garlic, minced or pressed
- ⅓ cup bulgur
- 2 cups low-sodium chicken broth
- 2 tablespoons reduced-sodium soy sauce

1. Heat oil in a wide nonstick frying pan over medium-high heat. Add carrots, zucchini, bell pepper, and garlic; cook, stirring, until vegetables are soft (about 5 minutes).

2. Stir in bulgur, broth, and soy sauce. Bring to a boil over high heat; then cover, remove from heat, and let stand until liquid has been absorbed and bulgur is tender to bite (about 20 minutes). Serve warm or at room temperature. If made ahead, cover and refrigerate for up to 2 days. Makes about 10 servings.

Per serving: 51 calories (23% calories from fat), 2 g protein, 9 g carbohydrates, 1 g total fat (0.2 g saturated fat), 0 mg cholesterol, 141 mg sodium

Green Rice with Pistachios

Preparation time: About 15 minutes

Cooking time: About 1 hour

Looking for a new way to serve rice? Try this colorful side dish. Start by oven-toasting the rice; then simmer it in broth with green peppercorns, spinach, and parsley. A sprinkling of pistachios adds a crunchy finishing touch.

- 2 cups long-grain white rice
- 5½ cups low-sodium chicken broth
- ½ teaspoon ground nutmeg
- 1½ tablespoons canned green peppercorns in brine, rinsed and drained
- 12 ounces stemmed spinach leaves, rinsed well, drained, and finely chopped (about 3 cups lightly packed)
- 1 cup minced parsley
  Salt and pepper
- ½ cup shelled salted roasted pistachio nuts, coarsely chopped

1. Spread rice in a shallow 3- to 3½-quart baking dish (about 9 by 13 inches). Bake in a 350° oven, stirring occasionally, until rice is lightly browned (about 35 minutes).

2. In a 2- to 3-quart pan, combine 5 cups of the broth, nutmeg, and peppercorns. Bring to a boil over high heat. Leaving baking dish on oven rack, carefully stir broth mixture into rice. Cover dish tightly with foil. Continue to bake until liquid has been absorbed and rice is tender to bite (about 20 more minutes). Stir after 10 and 15 minutes, covering dish again after stirring.

3. Uncover baking dish and stir in remaining ½ cup broth, spinach, and ¾ cup of the parsley; bake for 5 more minutes. To serve, stir rice and season to taste with salt and pepper. Sprinkle with remaining ¼ cup parsley and pistachios. Makes 8 to 10 servings.

Per serving: 226 calories (21% calories from fat), 7 g protein, 38 g carbohydrates, 5 g total fat (1 g saturated fat), 0 mg cholesterol, 123 mg sodium

Mexican Rice

Preparation time: About 10 minutes

Cooking time: About 35 minutes

White rice seasoned with tomatoes and chiles is a superb accompaniment for your favorite Mexican-style entrées. Try it with Turkey Chorizo Enchiladas (page 20) or Jalapeño Chicken with Mole Poblano (page 59), for example.

  1 **large can (about 28 oz.) tomatoes**
     About 3 cups low-sodium chicken broth
  2 **teaspoons butter or margarine**
  2 **cups long-grain white rice**
  1 **large onion, chopped**
  2 **cloves garlic, minced or pressed**
  2 **medium-size fresh green Anaheim or other large mild chiles (about 4 oz. *total*), seeded and chopped; or 1 small can (about 4 oz.) diced green chiles**
     Salt and pepper
  ¼ **cup firmly packed cilantro leaves**

1. Drain liquid from tomatoes into a glass measure. Add enough of the broth to make 4 cups liquid. Set tomatoes and broth mixture aside.

2. Melt butter in a 4- to 6-quart pan over medium-high heat. Add rice and cook, stirring, until it begins to turn opaque (about 3 minutes). Add onion, garlic, chiles, and ¼ cup water; continue to cook, stirring, for 5 more minutes. Add more water, 1 tablespoon at a time, if pan appears dry.

3. Add tomatoes and broth mixture to pan (break tomatoes up with a spoon). Bring to a boil over medium-high heat; then reduce heat, cover, and simmer until liquid has been absorbed and rice is tender to bite (about 25 minutes).

4. To serve, season to taste with salt and pepper; garnish with cilantro. Makes 10 to 12 servings.

Per serving: 163 calories (9% calories from fat), 4 g protein, 33 g carbohydrates, 2 g total fat (1 g saturated fat), 2 mg cholesterol, 142 mg sodium

Lemon-Caper Rice

Preparation time: About 5 minutes

Cooking time: About 25 minutes

Tangy with lemon and vinegar, this easy-to-make side dish is delicious with any simply cooked main course. You might serve it with Carne Asada (page 52) or Whole Tilapia with Onion & Lemon (page 64).

  6 **slices bacon**
  1 **cup short- or medium-grain rice**
  1 **tablespoon grated lemon peel**
  2½ **cups water**
  3 **tablespoons drained capers**
  ¼ **cup seasoned rice vinegar; or ¼ cup distilled white vinegar plus 1½ teaspoons sugar**

1. Cook bacon in a 2- to 3-quart pan over medium heat until crisp (about 5 minutes). Lift out, drain, crumble, and set aside. Discard all but 2 teaspoons of the drippings.

2. To pan, add rice, lemon peel, and water. Bring to a boil over high heat. Stir; then reduce heat, cover, and simmer until liquid has been absorbed and rice is tender to bite (about 20 minutes). Uncover; stir in crumbled bacon, capers, and vinegar. Makes 6 to 8 servings.

Per serving: 150 calories (23% calories from fat), 4 g protein, 24 g carbohydrates, 4 g total fat (1 g saturated fat), 5 mg cholesterol, 357 mg sodium

To make Roasted Chiles with Eggs (recipe on page 84), start by roasting
and peeling fresh poblano chiles; then stuff them with a mild blend of eggs,
spinach, and cottage cheese. Add warm rolls and you have a
wonderful light entrée for brunch, lunch, or supper.

E G G S

C H E E S E

With a little lightening-up, Mexican-style egg

and cheese dishes can easily join your list of lean

favorites. These recipes are versatile, too—you'll want

to try Drowned Eggs and Fiesta Brunch Casseroles

for lunch or dinner as well as at breakfast. Even our

berry-filled burritos, designed for a morning meal on

the run, are marvelous for noontime snacking.

Pictured on page 82

Roasted Chiles with Eggs

Preparation time: About 20 minutes

Cooking time: About 10 minutes

For a leaner twist on a classic favorite, these chiles are roasted, not battered and fried—and they're stuffed with thyme-accented eggs instead of cheese. You can use stubby poblanos, slender Anaheims, or any other large chile suitable for stuffing.

Roasted Chiles (directions follow)

1 cup Lime Salsa (page 33)

2 large eggs

4 large egg whites

½ cup *each* nonfat cottage cheese and finely chopped spinach leaves

1 tablespoon thinly sliced green onion

2 teaspoons cornstarch blended with 1 tablespoon cold water

1½ teaspoons fresh thyme leaves or ¼ teaspoon dry thyme

⅛ teaspoon *each* salt and white pepper

1 teaspoon salad oil

Sliced fresh hot red chiles (seeded, if desired)

Thyme sprigs

About ¾ cup plain nonfat yogurt

Thinly sliced green onion

1. Prepare Roasted Chiles; set aside. Prepare Lime Salsa; refrigerate.

2. In a food processor, whirl eggs, egg whites, cottage cheese, spinach, the 1 tablespoon onion, cornstarch mixture, thyme leaves, salt, and white pepper until smoothly puréed. (Or place ingredients in a bowl and beat with a spoon until well blended.) Set aside.

3. Heat oil in a medium-size nonstick frying pan over medium heat. Add egg mixture to pan; stir to combine. Cook until mixture is softly set and looks like scrambled eggs (3 to 5 minutes).

4. Spoon hot egg mixture equally into chiles. Place filled chiles on a platter and garnish with red chile slices and thyme sprigs. Add yogurt, thinly sliced onion, and Lime Salsa to taste. Makes 4 servings.

Roasted Chiles. Place 4 **fresh green poblano or Anaheim chiles** (or other large mild chiles) on a 12- by 15-inch baking sheet. Broil 4 to 6 inches below heat, turning often, until charred all over (5 to 8 minutes). Cover with foil and let cool on baking sheet; then remove and discard skins. Cut a slit down one side of each chile, but do not cut all the way to stem end and tip; be careful not to puncture opposite side of chile. Remove and discard seeds and veins from chiles.

Per serving: 138 calories (26% calories from fat), 14 g protein, 11 g carbohydrates, 4 g total fat (1 g saturated fat), 110 mg cholesterol, 298 mg sodium

Chiles Rellenos Casserole

Preparation time: About 25 minutes

Cooking time: 1 to 1¼ hours

This light casserole-style version of popular *chiles rellenos* is lacking in fat and calories—but not in flavor. The chiles are filled with high-protein tofu and just a small amount of cheese.

2 cups Red Chile Sauce (page 19) or Cherry Tomato Salsa (page 32)

About 1 pound soft tofu, rinsed

1 cup (about 4 oz.) shredded reduced-fat jack cheese

2 large cans (about 7 oz. *each*) whole green chiles

2 large eggs

6 large egg whites

⅔ cup nonfat milk

1 cup all-purpose flour

1 teaspoon baking powder

¾ cup shredded reduced-fat Cheddar cheese

Sliced ripe olives (optional)

1. Prepare Red Chile Sauce; set aside.

2. Coarsely mash tofu with a fork or your fingers; place in a colander and let drain for 10 minutes. Transfer to a bowl and mix in jack cheese. Cut a slit down one side of each chile; fill chiles equally with tofu mixture and arrange side by side in a lightly oiled shallow 2½- to 3-quart casserole.

3. In a large bowl, beat eggs and egg whites with an electric mixer on high speed until thick and foamy. Add milk, flour, and baking powder; beat until smooth. Fold in a third of the Cheddar cheese. Pour egg mixture over chiles; sprinkle with remaining Cheddar cheese.

4. Bake in a 375° oven until top is a rich golden brown (30 to 40 minutes). Scatter olives over casserole, if desired. Spoon onto plates and accompany with warm Red Chile Sauce. Makes 8 servings.

Per serving: 257 calories (29% calories from fat), 17 g protein, 29 g carbohydrates, 8 g total fat (3 g saturated fat), 71 mg cholesterol, 603 mg sodium

Drowned Eggs

Preparation time: About 10 minutes

Cooking time: About 25 minutes

Eggs poached in a tomato sauce enriched with fiery serrano chiles, onions, and spices make a great one-pan meal.

>   1   **can (about 14½ oz.) tomatoes**
>   2   **cloves garlic, peeled**
>   ¾   **cup water**
>   2   **teaspoons chili powder**
> 1½   **teaspoons *each* dry oregano and sugar**
>   4   **large eggs**
>   ¼   **cup thinly sliced green onions**
>   4   **fresh serrano chiles, halved and seeded**
>   2   **tablespoons cilantro leaves**
>   **Salt and pepper**
>   8   **warm corn tortillas (page 25)**

1. Pour tomatoes and their liquid into a blender or food processor. Add garlic, then whirl until smoothly puréed.

2. Transfer tomato purée to a wide frying pan. Stir in water, chili powder, oregano, and sugar; bring to a boil over medium-high heat. Reduce heat so sauce is simmering. Carefully crack eggs, one at a time, into sauce. Distribute onions and chile halves over sauce, disturbing eggs as little as possible. Cook, carefully basting eggs occasionally with sauce, until yolks are set to your liking (about 20 minutes for firm but moist yolks).

3. Divide eggs, onions, chile halves, and sauce equally among 4 shallow (about 1½-cup size) casseroles. Sprinkle with cilantro; season to taste with salt and pepper. Serve with tortillas. Makes 4 servings.

Per serving: 219 calories (27% calories from fat), 11 g protein, 31 g carbohydrates, 7 g total fat (2 g saturated fat), 213 mg cholesterol, 326 mg sodium

Corn Pudding

Preparation time: About 15 minutes

Cooking time: 70 to 80 minutes

Dotted with fresh corn kernels and diced red bell pepper, this comforting pudding makes an attractive company entrée. You might serve it with White Gazpacho (page 38).

>   7   **medium-size ears corn (about 3½ lbs. *total*), *each* about 8 inches long, husks and silk removed**
>   2   **teaspoons butter or margarine**
>   3   **ounces Neufchâtel or cream cheese**
>   ⅓   **cup all-purpose flour**
> 2¼   **cups nonfat milk**
>   ½   **cup diced red bell pepper**
>   ¼   **teaspoon *each* ground red pepper (cayenne) and salt**
>   2   **large eggs**
>   4   **large egg whites**

1. Toast corn ears, a few at a time, in a wide nonstick frying pan over medium heat until a third of the kernels on each ear are tinged with brown (about 15 minutes). Remove from heat; let cool.

2. With a sharp knife, cut corn kernels off cobs directly into frying pan. With dull side of knife, scrape cobs lengthwise so juices fall into pan. Add butter and Neufchâtel cheese. Cook over medium heat, stirring, until butter and cheese are melted. Sprinkle flour over corn mixture in pan and stir until blended. Remove from heat and stir in milk, bell pepper, ground red pepper, and salt.

3. In a medium-size bowl, beat eggs and egg whites until well blended; then stir eggs into corn mixture. Pour mixture into a buttered 2-inch-deep 8- by 12-inch baking dish. Bake in a 350° oven until center of pudding feels firm when pressed and edges are browned (55 to 65 minutes). Let stand for about 10 minutes before serving. Makes 12 servings.

Per serving: 112 calories (28% calories from fat), 6 g protein, 15 g carbohydrates, 4 g total fat (2 g saturated fat), 43 mg cholesterol, 155 mg sodium

Egg & Bean Burritos

Preparation time: About 25 minutes

Cooking time: About 40 minutes

Get your day off to a hearty start with these high-protein burritos. Refried beans and scrambled eggs seasoned with salsa, chiles, and cilantro make a delicious filling for flour tortillas.

  ¾ cup Cherry Tomato Salsa (page 32) or other salsa of your choice

1½ cups (about half a recipe) Zesty Refried Beans (page 57); or 1½ cups purchased nonfat refried beans

  1 small can (about 4 oz.) diced green chiles

  4 large eggs

  4 large egg whites

  1 teaspoon cornstarch

  ⅓ cup chopped cilantro

  6 warm flour tortillas (page 25)

  ½ cup shredded jack cheese

  1 cup plain nonfat yogurt

     Lime wedges

1. Prepare Cherry Tomato Salsa; refrigerate.

2. Prepare Zesty Refried Beans. Place beans in a wide nonstick frying pan and add chiles; cook over medium heat, stirring often, until bubbly (3 to 4 minutes). Meanwhile, in a large bowl, beat eggs, egg whites, and cornstarch until well blended. Stir in cilantro and 3 tablespoons of the salsa.

3. Push beans to one side of pan. Pour egg mixture into cleared area and cook over medium to medium-high heat, stirring often, until eggs are softly set (about 4 minutes).

4. For each burrito, spoon a sixth each of the beans and eggs in center of a tortilla; sprinkle with a sixth of the cheese, then roll to enclose. Serve each burrito, seam side down, on a warm plate. Add yogurt and remaining salsa to taste; garnish with lime wedges. Makes 6 servings.

Per serving: 312 calories (28% calories from fat), 18 g protein, 38 g carbohydrates, 10 g total fat (2 g saturated fat), 151 mg cholesterol, 739 mg sodium

---

Pictured on facing page

Fiesta Brunch Casseroles

Preparation time: About 10 minutes

Baking time: About 30 minutes

Individual egg, bean, and sausage casseroles are a colorful choice for brunch or supper. Alongside, serve Tomatillo & Tomato Salad (page 45) or a selection of ripe fresh fruit.

  1 cup Cucumber & Jicama Salsa (page 32)

  2 cans (about 15 oz. *each*) pinto beans; or 4 cups cooked (about 2 cups dried) pinto beans

  4 ounces ground turkey sausage, crumbled

  3 medium-size thin-skinned potatoes (about 1 lb. *total*), cooked, peeled, and diced

  2 teaspoons minced fresh basil or ½ teaspoon dry basil

     About ⅛ teaspoon pepper

  4 large eggs

  ⅓ cup shredded Cheddar cheese

  4 green onions, ends trimmed

  8 warm flour tortillas (page 25)

1. Prepare Cucumber & Jicama Salsa; refrigerate.

2. Drain beans, reserving ½ cup of the liquid from cans. Pour half the beans into a bowl; add reserved liquid (if using home-cooked beans, add ½ cup low-sodium chicken broth mixed with 1 teaspoon cornstarch). Mash beans until fairly smooth. Stir in remaining beans, sausage, potatoes, basil, and ⅛ teaspoon of the pepper.

3. Divide bean mixture equally among 4 shallow 2-cup casseroles. Set casseroles in one or two 10- by 15-inch rimmed baking pans. Bake in a 400° oven for about 10 minutes. Stir; bake for 5 more minutes, then remove from oven.

4. With the back of a spoon, impress an egg-size hollow in center of bean mixture in each casserole. Break an egg into each hollow. Sprinkle cheese equally over bean mixture. Return casseroles in pan(s) to oven and continue to bake until egg yolks are set to your liking (about 15 more minutes for firm but moist yolks). Garnish each casserole with an onion. Serve with tortillas; add salsa and pepper to taste. Makes 4 servings.

Per serving: 511 calories (23% calories from fat), 28 g protein, 71 g carbohydrates, 13 g total fat (5 g saturated fat), 244 mg cholesterol, 1,004 mg sodium

Delight your houseguests with this wake-up breakfast: warm tortillas, creamy Pineapple Rum Punch (recipe on page 113), and Fiesta Brunch Casseroles (recipe on facing page) to top with Cucumber & Jicama Salsa (recipe on page 32).

Red Pepper Flan

Preparation time: *About 20 minutes*

Baking time: *25 to 35 minutes*

For a satisfying lunch, choose savory flan instead of a sandwich. Infused with the subtle flavor of roasted red peppers, the delicate custard is enhanced by zesty Black Bean & Jicama Salad.

> 2 jars (about 7 oz. *each*) roasted red peppers, drained and patted dry (about 1 cup peppers *total*)
> 3 large eggs
> ⅓ cup low-sodium chicken broth
> Black Bean & Jicama Salad (page 76)
> Cilantro sprigs
> Salt and pepper

1. In a blender or food processor, combine red peppers, eggs, and broth; whirl until smoothly puréed. Pour purée equally into four ¾-cup ramekins or baking dishes (about 2 inches deep). Set ramekins, side by side, in a larger pan (at least 2 inches deep). Set pan on middle rack of a 325° oven.

2. Pour boiling water into larger pan up to level of pepper mixture. Bake until center of flan no longer jiggles when ramekins are gently shaken (25 to 35 minutes). Lift ramekins from water. Serve hot or cool. If made ahead, let cool completely; then cover and refrigerate until next day.

3. Prepare Black Bean & Jicama Salad; refrigerate until ready to serve or for up to 4 hours. To serve, set each ramekin on a plate; serve salad alongside. Garnish with cilantro sprigs; season to taste with salt and pepper. Makes 4 servings.

Per serving: 246 calories (23% calories from fat), 15 g protein, 33 g carbohydrates, 7 g total fat (3 g saturated fat), 167 mg cholesterol, 166 mg sodium

Spiced Bell Pepper Soufflés

Preparation time: *About 15 minutes*

Cooking time: *40 to 45 minutes*

Airy individual soufflés, each baked in a shiny bell pepper, are a nice choice for a brunch or light luncheon entrée.

> 6 large red, yellow, or green bell peppers (about 8 oz. *each*); choose squarish peppers that stand upright
> 1 teaspoon salad oil
> ¼ cup thinly sliced green onions
> ¾ cup low-sodium chicken broth
> 1 tablespoon cornstarch
> 3 tablespoons grated Parmesan cheese
> 1 tablespoon minced fresh oregano or 1 teaspoon dry oregano
> ⅛ teaspoon pepper
> 1 large egg yolk
> 5 large egg whites
> ½ teaspoon cream of tartar
> ⅛ teaspoon salt

1. If any of the peppers tips when set on its base, trim a thin slice from base (without piercing wall) so pepper sits steadily. Cut off top of each pepper about ¾ inch below base of stem (pepper shell needs to be about 2½ inches tall). Seed peppers, rinse, and set upright in a 9- by 13-inch baking pan. Cut out and discard stems from top pieces of peppers; then chop these pieces. Reserve ½ cup chopped peppers for soufflés; use remainder for soups or salads.

2. Heat oil in a small nonstick pan over medium-high heat. Add onions and the ½ cup chopped peppers; cook, stirring often, until vegetables are soft (about 4 minutes). If pan appears dry, add water, 1 teaspoon at a time.

3. In a small bowl, smoothly blend broth and cornstarch; add to pan along with cheese, oregano, and pepper. Bring sauce just to a boil over medium-high heat, stirring constantly. Then cook, stirring, just until slightly thickened. Remove from heat. In a bowl, whisk egg yolk just until blended; whisk in a little of the hot sauce, then whisk egg yolk mixture back into sauce in pan. Return to heat and stir just until sauce is bubbly. Let cool completely. (At this point, you may cover and refrigerate sauce and pepper shells separately until next day. Stir sauce until smooth before using.)

4. In a deep bowl, beat egg whites with an electric mixer on high speed until frothy. Add cream of tartar and salt and beat until whites hold firm, moist peaks. Stir about a third of the whites into sauce, then fold all of sauce into whites.

5. Gently pile soufflé equally into peppers. Bake, uncovered, in a 375° oven until soufflés are puffy and well browned (30 to 35 minutes). Serve immediately. Makes 6 servings.

Per serving: 94 calories (26% calories from fat), 6 g protein, 12 g carbohydrates, 3 g total fat (0.9 g saturated fat), 37 g cholesterol, 150 mg sodium

Fruit & Cheese Quesadillas

Preparation time: About 15 minutes

Baking time: 7 to 9 minutes

Even when you don't have much time to put together a meal, try to keep good nutrition in mind. These slightly sweet quesadillas, easy to assemble in just a few minutes, make a satisfying, lowfat breakfast or lunch.

½	**cup chopped dried apricots**
1	**teaspoon grated orange peel**
6	**tablespoons orange juice**
	About 2 cups part-skim ricotta cheese
	About 6 tablespoons honey, or to taste
1	**teaspoon ground coriander**
12	**flour tortillas (7- to 9-inch diameter)**
3	**cups chopped fresh or canned pineapple, drained well**
	Mint sprigs (optional)

1. In a bowl, combine apricots, orange peel, and orange juice; let stand until apricots are softened (about 10 minutes).

2. In a food processor or blender, combine apricot-juice mixture, ricotta cheese, honey, and coriander; whirl until smoothly puréed. (At this point, you may cover and refrigerate for up to 2 days.)

3. Arrange 6 tortillas in a single layer on 2 or 3 lightly oiled large baking sheets. Spread tortillas evenly with cheese mixture, covering tortillas to within ½ inch of edges. Evenly cover cheese mix-

ture with pineapple, then top each tortilla with one of the remaining tortillas; press lightly.

4. Bake in a 450° oven until tortillas are lightly browned (7 to 9 minutes), switching positions of baking sheets halfway through baking.

5. Slide quesadillas onto a board; cut each into 4 to 6 wedges. Arrange on a platter and garnish with mint sprigs, if desired. Makes 8 to 10 servings.

Per serving: 312 calories (21% calories from fat), 10 g protein, 52 g carbohydrates, 8 g total fat (3 g saturated fat), 16 mg cholesterol, 288 mg sodium

Berry Ricotta Breakfast Burritos

Preparation time: About 5 minutes

Baking time: 5 to 8 minutes

Fresh fruit and ricotta cheese are wrapped in flour tortillas for an extra-easy morning meal.

2	**flour tortillas (7- to 9-inch diameter)**
¼	**cup part-skim ricotta cheese or Neufchâtel cheese**
1	**cup sliced hulled strawberries or whole raspberries**
	Sugar

1. Spread tortillas equally with ricotta cheese, then top equally with berries. Sprinkle with sugar to taste. Fold opposite sides of each tortilla over filling, then roll each from one end to enclose.

2. You may bake or microwave burritos.

To bake, arrange burritos, seam side down, on a nonstick baking sheet; brush lightly with water. Bake in a 350° oven until filling is hot in center (5 to 8 minutes).

To microwave, heat one burrito at a time: set a burrito, seam side down, on a microwave-safe plate and brush lightly with water. Microwave, uncovered, on **HIGH (100%)** for 1 to 2 minutes or until tortilla is hot to touch; check after 1 minute. Repeat to heat remaining burrito.

3. Let burritos cool slightly before eating. Makes 2 servings.

Per serving: 179 calories (26% calories from fat), 7 g protein, 26 g carbohydrates, 5 g total fat (2 g saturated fat), 10 mg cholesterol, 207 mg sodium

Hearty yellow cornmeal adds flavor and crunch to a trio of breads (from top): Anise Biscuits (recipe on page 93), Cornbread (recipe on page 92), and Chili Batter Bread (recipe on page 92).

BREADS

PASTRIES

Cornbread, muffins, whole-grain loaves, moist raisin bread, classic Bolillos—you'll find them all here. Some of our breads are flavored with chiles and cheese; others gain crunch and color from yellow or blue cornmeal. Still others appeal with their special shapes—what bread-lover could resist top-hatted Semitas or a big wreath of Three Kings Bread?

Pictured on page 90

Chili Batter Bread

Preparation time: About 10 minutes

Baking time: About 30 minutes

Cornmeal gives this quick batter bread a light crunch; green chiles and a touch of chili powder add lively flavor.

- 2½ **cups all-purpose flour**
- ½ **cup yellow cornmeal**
- 3 **tablespoons sugar**
- 1 **teaspoon** *each* **chili powder and baking powder**
- ½ **teaspoon baking soda**
- ¼ **teaspoon salt**
- 1 **cup lowfat buttermilk**
- 1 **small can (about 4 oz.) diced green chiles**
- 1 **large egg white**

1. In a large bowl, mix flour, cornmeal, sugar, chili powder, baking powder, baking soda, and salt. Add buttermilk, chiles, and egg white; beat just until dry ingredients are evenly moistened. Scrape batter into a 10- by 15-inch nonstick (or lightly greased regular) rimmed baking pan. With a spatula, spread batter out to a 7-inch round.

2. Bake bread in a 375° oven until golden brown (about 30 minutes). Serve warm or cool, cut into wedges. If made ahead, wrap cooled loaf airtight and store at room temperature until next day (freeze for longer storage). Makes 1 loaf (12 to 14 servings).

Per serving: 132 calories (5% calories from fat), 4 g protein, 27 g carbohydrates, 1 g total fat (0 g saturated fat), 1 mg cholesterol, 207 mg sodium

Pictured on page 90

Cornbread

Preparation time: About 5 minutes

Baking time: About 30 minutes

A perfect accompaniment to spicy Mexican dishes, this mildly sweet yellow cornbread is especially easy to make. If you prefer a nippier flavor, add diced green chiles to the batter.

- 1 **cup** *each* **yellow cornmeal and all-purpose flour**
- 4 **teaspoons baking powder**
- ¼ **teaspoon salt**
- 1 **large egg**
- 2 **large egg whites**
- 1 **cup lowfat buttermilk**
- 3 **tablespoons honey**
- 2 **tablespoons butter or margarine, melted**

1. In a large bowl, mix cornmeal, flour, baking powder, and salt. In a small bowl, beat egg, egg whites, buttermilk, honey, and butter until blended. Add egg mixture to flour mixture and stir just until dry ingredients are evenly moistened.

2. Spread batter in an 8-inch-square nonstick (or greased regular) baking pan. Bake in a 375° oven until bread pulls away from sides of pan and a wooden pick inserted in center comes out clean (about 30 minutes). Cut into 8 pieces (*each* 2 by 4 inches). Makes 8 servings.

Per serving: 200 calories (20% calories from fat), 6 g protein, 34 g carbohydrates, 4 g total fat (2 g saturated fat), 36 mg cholesterol, 396 mg sodium

Chile Cornbread

Follow directions for **Cornbread,** but stir 1 large can (about 7 oz.) **diced green chiles** into egg mixture before combining with flour mixture. Makes 8 servings.

Per serving: 206 calories (19% calories from fat), 6 g protein, 36 g carbohydrates, 4 g total fat (2 g saturated fat), 36 mg cholesterol, 547 mg sodium

Pictured on page 34

Cornhusk Muffins

Preparation time: About 20 minutes

Baking time: 25 to 35 minutes

Each of these flavorful cumin muffins bakes in its own decorative cornhusk wrapping. To keep the muffins moist and reduce the calorie count, we've replaced some of the fat with applesauce.

- 6 **to 8 dried cornhusks (*each* 6 to 8 inches long)**
- 2¼ **cups all-purpose flour**
- 2½ **teaspoons baking powder**
- ½ **teaspoon baking soda**
- 1 **tablespoon sugar**
- 1 **teaspoon cumin seeds**
- ⅓ **cup smooth unsweetened applesauce**
- 2 **tablespoons butter or margarine, cut into chunks**
- 1 **cup lowfat buttermilk**

1. Separate cornhusks and place in a large bowl. Pour boiling water over husks to cover; let soak until soft and pliable (about 10 minutes). Drain husks, pat dry, and tear lengthwise into 1½- to 2-inch-wide strips.

2. In each of 11 greased 2½-inch muffin cups, place 2 or 3 cornhusk strips, crossing centers of strips at bottom of each cup so ends fan out around sides. Set aside.

3. In a large bowl, mix flour, baking powder, baking soda, sugar, and cumin seeds. With a pastry blender or 2 knives, cut in applesauce and butter until mixture resembles coarse crumbs. Add buttermilk to flour mixture; stir just until dry ingredients are evenly moistened.

4. Spoon about ¼ cup batter into each lined muffin cup (you may have to adjust cornhusk strips so they sit evenly in cups). Bake in a 375° oven until tops of muffins are golden (25 to 35 minutes). Serve hot or warm; remove and discard cornhusks before eating muffins. Makes 11 muffins.

Per muffin: 132 calories (19% calories from fat), 4 g protein, 23 g carbohydrates, 3 g total fat (1 g saturated fat), 7 mg cholesterol, 213 mg sodium

Pictured on page 90

Anise Biscuits

Preparation time: About 10 minutes

Baking time: About 20 minutes

Tender, slightly sweet drop biscuits flavored with anise are delicious with jam at breakfast time, and just as good in place of dinner rolls.

- 1⅓ **cups all-purpose flour**
- ⅓ **cup yellow cornmeal**
- 2 **tablespoons sugar**
- 1½ **teaspoons baking powder**
- ¼ **teaspoon salt**
- ½ **to ¾ teaspoon anise seeds, crushed**
- ½ **cup nonfat milk**
- 2 **tablespoons *each* water and salad oil**
- 2 **large egg whites**
- ½ **teaspoon vanilla**

1. In a large bowl, mix flour, cornmeal, sugar, baking powder, salt, and anise seeds (use the ¾-teaspoon amount for a stronger anise flavor). In a small bowl, beat milk, water, oil, egg whites, and vanilla until blended. Add egg mixture to flour mixture; stir just until dry ingredients are evenly moistened.

2. Spoon batter in 14 equal mounds (*each* about 4-teaspoon size) on two 12- by 15-inch nonstick (or lightly greased regular) baking sheets, spacing mounds 2 inches apart. Bake in a 375° oven until biscuits are firm to the touch and lightly browned (about 20 minutes), switching positions of baking sheets halfway through baking. Serve warm or cool. Makes 14 biscuits.

Per biscuit: 86 calories (23% calories from fat), 2 g protein, 14 g carbohydrates, 2 g total fat (0.3 g saturated fat), 0.2 mg cholesterol, 104 mg sodium

Double Corn Biscuits

Preparation time: About 20 minutes

Baking time: About 1¼ hours

Though inspired by Italian *biscotti*, these twice-baked treats are savory, not sweet. Flavored with Parmesan and cumin, they're delicious with Creamy Guacamole (page 29), fresh fruit, or Corn Salsa (page 33).

  ⅔ **cup all-purpose flour**
  ⅓ **cup grated Parmesan cheese**
  ¼ **cup yellow cornmeal**
  2 **tablespoons sugar**
  ½ **teaspoon *each* baking powder and salt**
  ¼ **teaspoon *each* baking soda and ground cumin**
  1 **cup fresh-cut yellow or white corn kernels (from 1 large ear corn); or 1 cup frozen corn kernels, thawed**
  1 **large egg**
  1 **large egg white**

1. In a small bowl, mix flour, cheese, cornmeal, sugar, baking powder, salt, baking soda, and cumin; set aside.

2. In a food processor, whirl corn until coarsely chopped (or chop corn with a knife and place in a large bowl). Add egg and egg white; whirl (or beat) just until blended. Add flour mixture and whirl (or stir) just until dry ingredients are evenly moistened.

3. Scrape dough directly onto a 12- by 15-inch nonstick (or lightly greased regular) baking sheet. With a spatula or floured fingers, shape dough into a flat loaf about 1½ inches thick and 2 inches wide; keep loaf 1 inch from ends of baking sheet.

4. Bake loaf in a 325° oven until firm to the touch (about 25 minutes). Remove from oven and let stand until cool enough to touch; then cut loaf crosswise on baking sheet into ½-inch-thick slices. Spread slices apart. Bake in a 300° oven until slices are lightly toasted all over (about 50 minutes). Transfer to racks and let cool. Makes about 2 dozen biscuits.

Per biscuit: 36 calories (16% calories from fat), 2 g protein, 6 g carbohydrates, 0.7 g total fat (0.3 g saturated fat), 10 mg cholesterol, 95 mg sodium

---

Pictured on facing page

Easy Corn-Cheese Bread

Preparation time: About 15 minutes

Rising time: About 45 minutes

Baking time: About 45 minutes

This hearty no-knead yeast bread gets its pleasantly moist texture from cottage cheese.

  1 **cup fresh-cut yellow or white corn kernels (from 1 large ear corn); or 1 cup frozen corn kernels, thawed**
  1 **cup beer**
  ½ **cup lowfat (2%) cottage cheese**
  ¼ **cup sugar**
  1 **package active dry yeast**
  ¼ **cup grated Parmesan cheese**
  ½ **teaspoon *each* salt and pepper**
    About 3¼ cups bread flour or all-purpose flour

1. Place corn in a fine wire strainer; press firmly with the back of a spoon to express liquid. Discard liquid; let corn drain well.

2. In a small pan, combine beer and cottage cheese. Heat over low heat until warm (about 110°F). Add sugar and yeast; let stand until yeast is softened (about 5 minutes).

3. In a food processor (or a large bowl), combine yeast mixture, corn, Parmesan cheese, salt, and pepper. Gradually add 3¼ cups of the flour, about 1 cup at a time, to make a soft dough; whirl (or beat) to combine after each addition. If needed, stir in more flour, 1 tablespoon at a time. Whirl (or beat) until dough is stretchy (about 3 minutes in a food processor, about 5 minutes by hand).

4. Scrape dough into a greased 6-cup soufflé dish or an 8- or 9-inch cheesecake pan with a removable rim. Cover dish or pan with oiled plastic wrap and let dough rise in a warm place until almost doubled (about 45 minutes).

5. Bake loaf in a 350° oven until golden brown (about 45 minutes). Let cool on a rack for about 15 minutes. Run a knife between bread and sides of dish; then turn bread out of dish onto rack (or remove pan rim and let bread cool on rack). Serve warm or cool. Makes 1 loaf (16 to 20 servings).

Per serving: 114 calories (6% calories from fat), 4 g protein, 23 g carbohydrates, 1 g total fat (0.3 g saturated fat), 1 mg cholesterol, 110 mg sodium

For a simple breakfast, a light lunch, or a filling snack, offer
moist slices of Easy Corn-Cheese Bread (recipe on facing page) with
a fresh fruit salad.

COOKIES

Wholesome grains and a variety of spices give these lowfat cookies appealing personality. Enjoy them for snacks or dessert, with glasses of milk or mugs of Mexican Hot Cocoa (page 113) or Mexican Coffee (page 112).

NOTE: To store cookies, package each kind separately in a rigid container. If cookies have frostings or toppings, or if they're sticky-textured, separate layers with wax paper. You can store cookies at room temperature for up to a day. After that, they'll begin to taste stale, so to hold them longer—even if just for a few days—freeze them. (You can serve them directly from the freezer.)

Pictured on page 98

MEXICAN WEDDING COOKIES

A lowfat, more cakelike version of Mexico's famous wedding cookies, these sugar-coated treats will delight guests of all ages on any occasion.

1½ cups all-purpose flour
1 teaspoon baking powder
¼ teaspoon salt
3 tablespoons butter or margarine, at room temperature
⅓ cup smooth unsweetened applesauce
About 1½ cups powdered sugar
1 large egg
1 teaspoon vanilla
¼ cup chopped pecans

1. In a small bowl, mix flour, baking powder, and salt. In a food processor (or in a large bowl), whirl (or beat) butter and applesauce until well blended. Add ½ cup of the sugar, egg, vanilla, and pecans; whirl (or beat) until smooth. Add flour mixture to egg mixture; whirl (or stir) until blended. Dough will be stiff.

2. With lightly floured fingers, shape 2-teaspoon portions of dough into balls; you should have 24. Set balls 1 inch apart on two 12- by 15-inch nonstick (or lightly greased regular) baking sheets. Bake in a 375° oven until cookies are light golden brown (about 15 minutes), switching positions of baking sheets halfway through baking. Let cool on baking sheets until lukewarm.

3. Sift ½ cup of the remaining sugar onto a large sheet of wax paper. Roll each cookie gently in sugar. With your fingers, pack more sugar all over each cookie to a depth of about ⅛ inch. Place cookies on a rack over wax paper and dust generously with remaining sugar; let cool completely. Makes 2 dozen cookies.

Per cookie: 84 calories (26% calories from fat), 1 g protein, 14 g carbohydrates, 3 g total fat (1 g saturated fat), 13 mg cholesterol, 60 mg sodium

ORANGE & COCOA COOKIES

To conclude a spicy meal on a sweet note, offer soft cookies filled with orange marmalade and drizzled with a cocoa glaze.

1½ cups all-purpose flour
1 teaspoon baking powder
¼ teaspoon salt
⅛ teaspoon ground cloves
2 tablespoons butter or margarine, at room temperature
¼ cup smooth unsweetened applesauce
½ cup powdered sugar
1 large egg
1 teaspoon vanilla
About ⅓ cup orange marmalade
Cocoa Glaze (recipe follows)

1. In a small bowl, mix flour, baking powder, salt, and cloves. In a food processor (or in a large bowl), whirl (or beat) butter and applesauce until well blended. Add sugar, egg, and vanilla; whirl (or beat) until smooth. Add flour mixture to egg mixture and whirl (or stir) until blended. Dough will be stiff.

2. With lightly floured fingers, shape 2-teaspoon portions of dough into balls. Set balls 1 inch apart on two 12- by 15-inch nonstick (or lightly greased regular) baking sheets. With floured thumb, press a well in center of each ball (don't press all the way through to baking sheet). Spoon about ½ teaspoon of the marmalade into each well (marmalade should not flow over rim).

3. Bake cookies in a 400° oven until light golden brown (about 15 minutes), switching positions of baking sheets halfway through baking. Let cookies cool on baking sheets for about 3 minutes; then transfer to racks to cool completely.

4. Prepare Cocoa Glaze. Set each rack of cookies over a baking sheet to catch any drips; drizzle warm glaze evenly over cookies. Serve warm; or let stand until glaze hardens (about 2 hours). Makes about 2 dozen cookies.

Cocoa Glaze. In a 1- to 1½-quart pan, combine ¼ cup **light corn syrup** and 1 tablespoon **unsweetened cocoa powder.** Cook over medium heat, stirring, just until mixture comes to a boil. Remove from heat and stir in ½ teaspoon **vanilla.** Use warm. Stir well before using.

Per cookie: 80 calories (14% calories from fat), 1 g protein, 16 g carbohydrates, 1 g total fat (1 g saturated fat), 11 mg cholesterol, 61 mg sodium

Pictured on page 98
COCOA PEPPER COOKIES

If you like spicy flavors, you'll applaud these unusual cookies. Crushed peppercorns add subtle heat and complement the cookies' sweetness.

- 1 **cup all-purpose flour**
- 2 **tablespoons unsweetened cocoa powder**
- 1 **teaspoon baking powder**
- 1 **cup sugar**
- 1 **teaspoon whole black peppercorns, coarsely crushed**
- 2 **tablespoons butter or margarine, melted**
- ⅓ **cup smooth unsweetened applesauce**
- ½ **teaspoon vanilla**
  Whole black peppercorns (optional)

1. In a food processor (or in a bowl), combine flour, cocoa, baking powder, ¾ cup of the sugar, and crushed peppercorns. Whirl (or stir) until blended. Add butter, applesauce, and vanilla; whirl until dough forms a compact ball. (Or stir in butter, applesauce, and vanilla with a fork, then work dough with your hands to form a smooth-textured ball.)

2. With lightly floured fingers, pinch off 1-inch pieces of dough and roll into balls. Arrange balls 2 inches apart on two 12- by 15-inch nonstick (or lightly greased regular) baking sheets. Dip bottom of a lightly greased glass into remaining ¼ cup sugar and press each ball gently to a thickness of about ½ inch; dip glass again as needed to prevent sticking. If desired, press a whole peppercorn in center of each cookie.

3. Bake in lower third of a 300° oven until cookies are firm to the touch and look dry on top (about 20 minutes), switching positions of baking sheets halfway through baking. Let cookies cool on baking sheets for about 3 minutes; then transfer to racks to cool completely. Makes about 1½ dozen cookies.

Per cookie: 84 calories (14% calories from fat), 0.7 g protein, 18 g carbohydrates, 1 g total fat (0.8 g saturated fat), 3 mg cholesterol, 41 mg sodium

Pictured on page 98
LEMON COOKIES

Rolled oats give these sweet-tart cookies a chewy texture.

- ½ **cup all-purpose flour**
- ¼ **teaspoon *each* baking soda and salt**
- ⅛ **teaspoon cream of tartar**
- 2 **tablespoons butter or margarine, at room temperature**
- 6 **tablespoons sugar**
- 2 **teaspoons lemon peel**
- ½ **teaspoon *each* lemon juice and vanilla**
- 1 **large egg white**
- ½ **cup regular rolled oats**
  Lemon Icing (recipe follows)

1. In a small bowl, mix flour, baking soda, salt, and cream of tartar. In a food processor (or in a large bowl), whirl (or beat) butter, sugar, lemon peel, lemon juice, vanilla, and egg white until well blended. Add flour mixture to egg mixture; whirl (or stir) until combined. Stir in oats.

2. With floured fingers, divide dough into 1½-teaspoon portions (you should have 18); place mounds of dough 2 inches apart on two 12- by 15-inch nonstick (or lightly greased regular) baking sheets.

3. Bake in a 350° oven until cookies are light golden and firm to the touch (about 15 minutes), switching positions of baking sheets halfway through baking. Let cookies cool on baking sheets for about 3 minutes; then transfer to racks to cool completely.

4. Prepare Lemon Icing. Set each rack of cookies over a baking sheet to catch any drips; drizzle icing evenly over cookies. Serve; or let stand until icing hardens (about 2 hours). Makes 1½ dozen cookies.

Lemon Icing. In a small bowl, combine ⅔ cup sifted **powdered sugar** and 2 teaspoons *each* **lemon juice** and **water.** Stir until smooth.

Per cookie: 50 calories (26% calories from fat), 0.9 g protein, 8 g carbohydrates, 1 g total fat (0.8 g saturated fat), 3 mg cholesterol, 64 mg sodium

Satisfy your sweet tooth with these tempting cookies (clockwise from right): Cocoa Pepper Cookies (recipe on page 97), laced with crushed black peppercorns; cakelike, sugar-coated Mexican Wedding Cookies (recipe on page 96); and chewy Lemon Cookies (recipe on page 97).

Graham & Cornmeal Yeast Bread

Preparation time: About 20 minutes

Rising time: About 2 hours

Baking time: 45 to 50 minutes

Toasty graham flour, ground from the entire wheat kernel, combines with cornmeal and all-purpose flour in this hearty multigrain bread. You'll find graham flour in well-stocked super-markets and in natural-foods stores; it's coarser in texture than whole wheat flour, but the two types are interchangeable in baking.

> 2 **packages active dry yeast**
> 1½ **cups warm water (about 110°F)**
> 1 **cup evaporated milk**
> 2 **tablespoons honey**
> 1 **tablespoon salad oil**
> 1 **teaspoon salt**
> **About 3 cups all-purpose flour**
> 2 **cups graham flour or whole wheat flour**
> 1½ **cups yellow cornmeal**
> 1 **large egg, lightly beaten**

1. In a large bowl, combine yeast and warm water; let stand until yeast is softened (about 5 minutes). Stir in milk, honey, oil, salt, and 2½ cups of the all-purpose flour. Beat with a heavy spoon until dough is well mixed and slightly stretchy (8 to 10 minutes). Add graham flour and cornmeal; beat with spoon until dry ingredients are evenly moistened.

2. Cover bowl with oiled plastic wrap; let dough rise in a warm place until almost doubled (about 1½ hours). Punch dough down to release air.

3. To knead by hand, scrape dough out onto a board floured with about ½ cup all-purpose flour. Knead until elastic and no longer sticky (about 10 minutes), adding more flour as needed to prevent sticking.

To knead with a dough hook, beat on high speed until dough pulls cleanly from sides of bowl and is no longer sticky (about 10 minutes); if needed, add more all-purpose flour, 1 tablespoon at a time.

4. On floured board, divide dough in half. Shape each half into a 6-inch round; then place each round on a 12- by 15-inch nonstick (or greased regular) baking sheet. Cover lightly with oiled plastic wrap and let rise in a warm place until puffy (about 30 minutes).

5. Brush loaves with egg and bake in a 350° oven until richly browned (45 to 50 minutes), switching positions of baking sheets halfway through baking. Let loaves cool on racks; serve warm or cool. If made ahead, wrap cooled loaves airtight and store at room temperature until next day (freeze for longer storage). Makes 2 loaves (10 to 12 servings *each*).

Per serving: 165 calories (12% calories from fat), 5 g protein, 31 g carbohydrates, 2 g total fat (1 g saturated fat), 13 mg cholesterol, 117 mg sodium

Bolillos

Preparation time: About 30 minutes

Rising time: About 2 hours

Baking time: 35 to 45 minutes

It's no coincidence that *bolillos*—crusty on the outside, soft on the inside—so closely resemble French bread: the French introduced these and other baked goods to Mexico in the 19th century. Perfect as dinner rolls, bolillos are also great for sandwiches—just split them, then fill with condiments and any meat or chicken filling.

- 2 **cups water**
- 1½ **tablespoons sugar**
- 1 **tablespoon salt**
- 2 **tablespoons butter or margarine**
- 1 **package active dry yeast**
  About 6 cups all-purpose flour
- 1 **teaspoon cornstarch**
- ½ **cup water**

1. In a small pan, combine the 2 cups water, sugar, salt, and butter; heat over low heat until warm (about 110°F). Pour into a large bowl and stir in yeast; let stand until yeast is softened (about 5 minutes). Add 5 cups of the flour and beat with a heavy spoon until blended. Then scrape dough out onto a floured board and knead until smooth and elastic (about 10 minutes), adding more flour as needed to prevent sticking. Place dough in an oiled bowl and turn over to grease top. Cover with oiled plastic wrap and let rise in a warm place until almost doubled (about 1½ hours).

2. Punch dough down to release air, turn out onto a lightly floured board, and knead briefly. Divide into 16 equal pieces. Form each piece into a smooth ball; then roll and gently pull each ball from center to ends to make an oblong about 4 inches long (center should be thicker than ends). Place rolls 2 inches apart on two 12- by 15-inch nonstick (or greased regular) baking sheets. Cover with oiled plastic wrap and let rise until almost doubled (about 35 minutes).

3. In a small pan, blend cornstarch and the ½ cup water. Bring to a boil; remove from heat and let cool slightly. Brush each roll with cornstarch mixture. With a sharp knife or razor blade, cut a lengthwise slash about ¾ inch deep and 2 inches long in top of each roll.

4. Bake in a 375° oven until rolls are golden brown and sound hollow when tapped on bottom (35 to 45 minutes), switching positions of baking sheets halfway through baking. Let cool on racks. If made ahead, wrap cooled rolls airtight and store at room temperature until next day (freeze for longer storage). Makes 16 rolls.

Per roll: 190 calories (9% calories from fat), 5 g protein, 37 g carbohydrates, 2 g total fat (1 g saturated fat), 4 mg cholesterol, 428 mg sodium

Semitas

Preparation time: About 25 minutes

Rising time: About 1¾ hours

Baking time: About 20 minutes

The state of Puebla is famous for its breads, among them the top-hatted rolls called *semitas*. The "hats" are lifted off the thick rolls to make way for sandwich fillings such as chili- and anise-spiced chicken (page 60), Tinga (page 24), or breaded veal cutlets.

If you can't find semolina flour and bread flour in your supermarket, check at a natural-foods store or gourmet shop.

- 2 **cups warm water (about 110°F)**
- 1 **package active dry yeast**
- 1 **tablespoon sugar**
- 1½ **teaspoons salt**
- 2 **cups bread flour or all-purpose flour**
- 2 **cups semolina flour**
- ⅓ **cup *each* masa harina (dehydrated masa flour) and yellow or white cornmeal; or ⅓ cup semolina flour plus ⅓ cup bread flour or all-purpose flour**
- 1½ **tablespoons salt blended with 3 tablespoons hot water**

1. In a large bowl, combine warm water, yeast, sugar, and the 1½ teaspoons salt; let stand until yeast is softened (about 5 minutes). In another bowl, mix the 2 cups bread flour, the 2 cups semolina flour, masa harina, and cornmeal. Stir 3 cups of this flour mixture into yeast mixture. Beat with a heavy spoon or an electric mixer until dough is stretchy.

2. Stir in remaining flour mixture (about 1⅔

cups); then beat with a dough hook or a heavy spoon until dough is elastic and only slightly sticky (8 to 10 minutes). Cover with oiled plastic wrap and let rise in a warm place until almost doubled (about 1 hour). Beat dough down with dough hook or spoon to release air. Scrape dough out onto a board lightly floured with bread flour or all-purpose flour; divide dough into 8 equal pieces.

3. Work with one piece of dough at a time. Knead each piece of dough to make a smooth ball. Gently roll and pull ball to elongate it. Press down on ball with the edge of your hand, forming a figure 8 with a third of the dough at one end and a "midriff" about ½ inch wide. Flatten figure 8 to ¼ inch thick. Gently lift smaller end, twist it over, and lay it on larger end. Gently press top piece to secure to base. As rolls are shaped, set them 2 inches apart on two 12- by 15-inch nonstick (or lightly greased regular) baking sheets. Let rise, uncovered, until puffy (about 45 minutes).

4. If you have only one oven, you'll need to bake rolls one sheet at a time. When rolls are ready to bake, brush one sheet of rolls with salt-water mixture; refrigerate second sheet until ready to bake. Set a large (about 12- by 15-inch) rimmed baking pan on lowest rack of a 450° oven; pour ½ inch boiling water into pan. Position remaining oven rack just above water and place sheet of rolls on rack. Bake rolls until richly browned (about 20 minutes). Repeat to bake second sheet of rolls. (If you have 2 ovens, you can simply duplicate the setup in second oven and bake all rolls at once.) Serve warm (rolls are best eaten when freshly baked). Or, if made ahead, let cool on racks; then wrap airtight and freeze. Makes 8 rolls.

Per roll: 284 calories (4% calories from fat), 9 g protein, 59 g carbohydrates, 1 g total fat (0.2 g saturated fat), 0 mg cholesterol, 1,649 mg sodium

hree Kings Bread

Preparation time: About 25 minutes

Rising time: About 40 minutes

Baking time: 35 to 40 minutes

Crown your table with Three Kings Bread—a fruit-laced yeast bread traditionally served in Mexico on Twelfth Night (January 6). The bread is baked in a ring and royally jeweled with fruits and nuts; a tiny ceramic doll or dried lima bean is baked inside. The guest who discovers the "treasure" is obliged to host another party on February 2, the Feast of Candelaria.

> ¼ cup *each* raisins and chopped dried or candied cherries (or use all raisins or all cherries)
> ¼ cup finely chopped walnuts
> About 3 cups all-purpose flour
> ¼ teaspoon salt
> 1 package active dry yeast
> 1 cup nonfat milk
> ¼ cup honey
> 2 tablespoons butter or margarine
> 1 large egg
> 1 teaspoon *each* grated lemon peel and grated orange peel
> Sugar Glaze (recipe follows)
> Dried or candied fruits and nuts

1. In a small bowl, combine raisins, cherries, and walnuts; set aside. In a large bowl, mix 1½ cups of the flour, salt, and yeast; set aside. In a small pan, heat milk, honey, and butter over medium heat until very warm (120° to 130°F).

2. *To mix and knead by hand,* gradually add milk mixture to flour mixture; beat with a heavy spoon until smooth. Add egg, lemon peel, and orange peel; beat until well blended. Add 1½ cups more flour and beat until dough is stretchy (about 5 minutes). Scrape dough out onto a lightly floured board and knead until smooth and satiny (8 to 10 minutes), adding more flour as needed to prevent sticking.

To mix and knead in a food processor, combine milk mixture and flour mixture in work bowl of food processor; whirl to combine. Add egg, lemon peel, and orange peel; whirl to blend. Add 1½ cups more flour and whirl for 1 minute; dough should pull from sides of work bowl and no longer feel sticky. If it's still sticky, add more flour, 1 tablespoon at a time, whirling just until incorporated after each addition.

3. On lightly floured board, pat dough out to make a 7-inch round. Top dough with raisin-nut mixture, fold up edges, and knead until fruits and nuts are evenly distributed. Then shape dough into a 24-inch-long roll (let dough rest for a few minutes between kneading and stretching if it's too elastic to stay in place). Carefully transfer roll to a lightly greased 12- by 15-inch nonstick baking sheet. Join ends to form a ring; pinch firmly to seal. Cover lightly with oiled plastic wrap and let rise in a warm place until almost doubled (about 40 minutes).

4. Bake in a 350° oven until bread is golden brown and sounds hollow when tapped on bottom (35 to 40 minutes). Carefully transfer bread from baking sheet to a rack and let cool almost completely. If made ahead, wrap cooled loaf airtight and store at room temperature until next day (freeze for longer storage).

5. To serve, prepare Sugar Glaze and drizzle evenly over loaf. Decorate with fruits and nuts. Makes 1 loaf (14 to 16 servings).

Sugar Glaze. In a bowl, combine 1 cup sifted **powdered sugar,** about 4 teaspoons **nonfat milk** (or a little more if needed for desired consistency), and ½ teaspoon **vanilla.** Stir until smooth.

Per serving: 192 calories (17% calories from fat), 4 g protein, 36 g carbohydrates, 4 g total fat (1 g saturated fat), 19 mg cholesterol, 67 mg sodium

Pictured on facing page

opaipillas

Preparation time: About 20 minutes

Rising time: 65 to 70 minutes

Cooking time: 50 to 55 minutes

Our tender sopaipillas are as crisp and chewy as the traditional deep-fried breads, but to slim down the recipe, we've changed the cooking technique: the pastries are first boiled, then baked. Serve these favorites hot from the oven, with honey or anise-scented syrup. Or, for a savory snack, fill split sopaipillas with Zesty Refried Beans (page 57) or Shredded Chicken Filling (page 56).

> 1   package active dry yeast
> ¼   cup warm water (about 110°F)
> 1½   cups nonfat milk
> 3   tablespoons solid vegetable shortening
> 1   teaspoon salt
> 3   tablespoons granulated sugar
>   About 4 cups all-purpose flour
>   Powdered sugar (optional)
>   Honey or flavored syrups (optional)

1. In a large bowl, combine yeast and warm water; let stand until yeast is softened (about 5

minutes). In a small pan, combine milk, shortening, salt, and 2 tablespoons of the granulated sugar; heat over low heat until warm (about 110°F), then stir into yeast mixture.

2. *To mix and knead by hand,* beat 4 cups of the flour into yeast mixture with a heavy spoon; continue to beat until dough is stretchy (about 5 minutes). Scrape dough out onto a floured board; knead until smooth and satiny (8 to 10 minutes), adding more flour as needed to prevent sticking.

To mix and knead in a food processor, combine yeast mixture and 4 cups of the flour in work bowl of a food processor. Whirl for 1 minute; dough should pull from sides of work bowl and no longer feel sticky. If it's still sticky, add more flour, 1 tablespoon at a time, whirling just until incorporated after each addition.

3. Place dough kneaded by either method in an oiled bowl and turn over to grease top. Cover with oiled plastic wrap and let rise in a warm place until almost doubled (about 45 minutes).

4. Punch dough down to release air, turn out onto a lightly floured board, and knead briefly. Divide dough into 4 equal pieces. Roll each piece out to about a 7-inch round. With a floured knife, cut each round into 6 equal pieces. Transfer to lightly floured baking sheets and cover with oiled plastic wrap. Let stand at room temperature until puffy (20 to 25 minutes).

5. Meanwhile, bring 3 quarts water and remaining 1 tablespoon granulated sugar to a boil in a large pan over high heat; adjust heat so water boils gently. Also lightly grease two 12- by 15-inch baking sheets.

6. Transfer puffy dough wedges, up to 5 at a time, to simmering water. Cook, turning often, for 4 minutes. With a slotted spoon, lift each piece from water and drain well. Set on prepared baking sheets. Bake in a 400° oven until golden brown (30 to 35 minutes), switching positions of baking sheets halfway through baking. Serve warm (sopaipillas are best eaten when freshly baked). Or, if made ahead, let cool on racks; then wrap airtight and freeze for up to 1 month. Thaw before reheating; reheat just until warm (if overheated, pastries will harden).

7. Dust warm sopaipillas liberally with powdered sugar and serve with honey, if desired. Makes 2 dozen sopaipillas.

Per sopaipilla: 102 calories (16% calories from fat), 3 g protein, 18 g carbohydrates, 2 g total fat (0.4 g saturated fat), 0.3 mg cholesterol, 100 mg sodium

Hot, puffy Sopaipillas (recipe on facing page), dusted with powdered sugar
and drizzled with honey, are delightful for breakfast or any-time snacking.
Serve them with big mugs of coffee or cappuccino.

BLUE CORNMEAL

A staple in Mexico, blue corn-meal is now available in most areas of the United States as well. It's entirely interchangeable with the familiar yellow or white meal, but it does add a distinctive parched-corn flavor to tortillas and other baked goods—such as the muffins and spoonbread presented here.

Blue cornmeal is sold in specialty food shops, natural-foods stores, and some well-stocked supermarkets; it's also available by mail-order (see page 124). Some sources offer both coarse and fine grinds; for the recipes on this page, use the more finely ground meal (*harina para atole*).

BLUE CORN MUFFINS

Corn muffins take on an interesting new look and flavor when they're made with blue cornmeal.

- 1 cup *each* blue cornmeal and all-purpose flour
- 2 tablespoons sugar
- 1 tablespoon baking powder
- ½ teaspoon salt
- 4 large egg whites
- 1 cup nonfat milk
- ⅓ cup smooth unsweetened applesauce

- 2 tablespoons butter or margarine, melted
  Honey
  Butter or margarine (optional)

1. In a large bowl, mix cornmeal, flour, sugar, baking powder, and salt. In another bowl, beat egg whites, milk, applesauce, and melted butter until blended. Add egg mixture to flour mixture and stir just until dry ingredients are evenly moistened.

2. Spoon batter into 12 paper-lined or greased 2½-inch muffin cups. Bake in a 400° oven until muffins are browned and a wooden pick inserted in centers comes out clean (about 20 minutes). Serve warm or cool, with honey and, if desired, butter. If made ahead, wrap cooled muffins airtight and store at room temperature until next day (freeze for longer storage). Makes 1 dozen muffins.

Per muffin: 121 calories (17% calories from fat), 4 g protein, 21 g carbohydrates, 2 g total fat (1 g saturated fat), 6 mg cholesterol, 262 mg sodium

BLUE CORN SPOONBREAD

Though it's made without oil, this quick spoonbread is nonetheless moist and rich-tasting. Fresh corn kernels give it a nice texture and a naturally sweet flavor.

- ½ cup *each* blue cornmeal and all-purpose flour
- 2 tablespoons sugar
- 1½ teaspoons baking powder
- ½ teaspoon ground coriander

- ¼ teaspoon *each* salt and pepper
- 1 cup nonfat milk
- 1 large egg
- 2 large egg whites
- ⅔ cup fresh-cut yellow or white corn kernels (from about 1 medium-size ear corn); or ⅔ cup frozen corn kernels, thawed

1. In a large bowl, mix cornmeal, flour, sugar, baking powder, coriander, salt, and pepper. In a small bowl, beat milk, egg, and egg whites until blended. Add egg mixture and corn to flour mixture and stir just until dry ingredients are evenly moistened.

2. Pour batter into a 9-inch nonstick (or lightly greased regular) pie or cake pan. Bake in a 400° oven until spoonbread is browned on top and a wooden pick inserted in center comes out clean (about 20 minutes). For best flavor, serve spoonbread freshly baked; spoon out of pan to serve. Makes 8 servings.

Per serving: 108 calories (9% calories from fat), 5 g protein, 20 g carbohydrates, 1 g total fat (0.3 g saturated fat), 27 mg cholesterol, 199 mg sodium

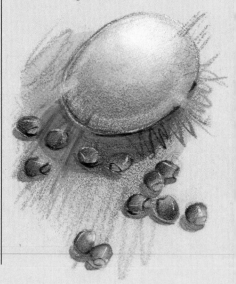

Pictured on page 122

Raisin Batter Bread

Preparation time: About 10 minutes

Baking time: About 1¼ hours

Breads and other baked goods are a national passion in Mexico. This delicate, slightly sweet raisin loaf offers all the fresh-baked goodness of its traditional counterpart, but it's missing much of the fat.

- 1 **large egg**
- 2 **large egg whites**
- 2 **tablespoons water**
- ⅔ **cup sugar**
- 5 **tablespoons butter or margarine, at room temperature**
- 1 **tablespoon grated orange peel**
- 1 **cup reduced-fat or regular sour cream (do not use nonfat sour cream)**
- 2 **cups bread flour or all-purpose flour**
- 2 **teaspoons baking powder**
- ½ **teaspoon baking soda**
- 1¼ **cups raisins**

1. In a large bowl, beat egg, egg whites, water, sugar, butter, and orange peel until blended. Stir in sour cream. In a small bowl, mix flour, baking powder, and baking soda; add to egg mixture and beat until blended. Stir in raisins.

2. Scrape batter into a lightly greased 5- by 9-inch nonstick loaf pan. Spread batter to smooth top. Bake in a 325° oven until bread begins to pull away from sides of pan and a wooden pick inserted in center comes out clean (about 1¼ hours). Let cool in pan on a rack for about 15 minutes. Run a knife between bread and sides of pan; then turn loaf out of pan onto rack to cool completely. If made ahead, wrap cooled loaf airtight and store at room temperature for up to 2 days (freeze for longer storage). Makes 1 loaf (10 to 12 servings).

Per serving: 276 calories (29% calories from fat), 6 g protein, 45 g carbohydrates, 9 g total fat (5 g saturated fat), 41 mg cholesterol, 217 mg sodium

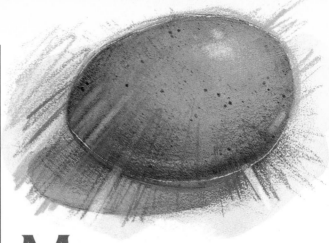

Mango Quick Bread

Preparation time: About 15 minutes

Baking time: 50 to 55 minutes

Mangoes, a favorite Mexican fruit, give this coconut-flecked quick bread its golden color and sweet flavor.

- 1 **cup puréed ripe mango (about a 1-lb. mango)**
- ¾ **teaspoon baking soda mixed with 2 teaspoons water**
- 1 **cup sugar**
- 2 **large eggs**
- ½ **cup sweetened flaked coconut, minced**
- ¼ **cup salad oil**
- 2½ **cups all-purpose flour**
- 1½ **teaspoons baking powder**

1. In a large bowl, stir together mango purée and baking soda mixture. Let stand for 5 minutes. Then add sugar, eggs, coconut, and oil; beat until blended. Stir together flour and baking powder; add to mango mixture and beat until very well blended.

2. Pour batter into a 5- by 9-inch nonstick (or lightly greased regular) loaf pan. Bake in a 350° oven until loaf is richly browned, begins to pull away from sides of pan, and springs back when pressed (50 to 55 minutes). Let cool in pan on a rack for about 10 minutes. Run a knife between bread and sides of pan; then turn loaf out of pan onto rack to cool completely. Serve warm or cool. If made ahead, wrap cooled loaf airtight and store at room temperature until next day (freeze for longer storage). Makes 1 loaf (10 to 12 servings).

Per serving: 266 calories (24% calories from fat), 4 g protein, 47 g carbohydrates, 7 g total fat (2 g saturated fat), 39 mg cholesterol, 174 mg sodium

For a perfect finish to any Mexican meal, offer a refreshing sweet soup such as Cactus Pear & Tree Pear Soup (right) or Sparkling Jewels Fruit Soup (left). Both recipes are on page 108.

DESSERTS

The favorite Mexican flavors of vanilla, cocoa, cinnamon, and citrus shine in these light desserts. Indulge your sweet tooth with moist, tender cakes, creamy flan, beautiful fruit soups, and warm, spicy rice or bread pudding. We've also included a selection of Mexican-style beverages, from chilly punches to fragrant hot coffee and cocoa.

Pictured on page 106

Cactus Pear & Tree Pear Soup

Preparation time: About 30 minutes

Cooking time: About 15 minutes

Two fruit purées—one vibrant magenta, the other pale yellow—are poured side by side into each individual bowl to create this dramatic, delectable dessert. The fruit of a native Mexican cactus, prickly pears (also called cactus pears or tunas) are available in the United States in Mexican markets and some well-stocked supermarkets from August through December. If you can't find them, substitute fresh or frozen raspberries.

> **Red Prickly Pear Purée or Raspberry Purée (recipes follow)**
> **Tree Pear Purée (recipe follows)**
> 6 **to 8 star anise (optional)**
> **Mint sprigs (optional)**

1. Prepare Red Prickly Pear Purée and Tree Pear Purée; pour each into a small pitcher.

2. With a pitcher in each hand, simultaneously and gently pour purées into an individual 1½- to 2-cup soup bowl (wide bowls create the most dramatic effect). Repeat to fill 5 to 7 more bowls, allowing a total of 1 to 1¼ cups purée for each serving. Garnish each serving with a star anise and mint sprigs, if desired. Makes 6 to 8 servings.

Red Prickly Pear Purée. Wearing rubber gloves to protect your hands from hidden needles, cut about 5 pounds despined **red prickly pears** (also called cactus pears or tunas) into halves lengthwise. Using a small knife, pull off and discard outer layer (including peel) from fruit; this layer will separate easily. Place fruit in a food processor (do not use a blender, which will pulverize seeds). Whirl until smoothly puréed, then pour into a fine strainer set over a bowl. Firmly rub purée through strainer into bowl; discard seeds. (Or rub purée through a food mill; discard seeds.)

To purée, add ⅓ cup **lemon juice** and 2 table-spoons **sugar**. If made ahead, cover and refrigerate until next day; stir before using.

Raspberry Purée. In a food processor, whirl 4 cups **fresh or frozen unsweetened raspberries**

until smoothly puréed (do not use a blender, which will pulverize seeds). Pour purée into a fine strainer set over a bowl. Firmly rub purée through strainer into bowl; discard seeds. (Or rub purée through a food mill; discard seeds.) To purée, add 1 cup **orange juice** and ⅓ cup *each* **lemon juice** and **sugar**. If made ahead, cover and refrigerate until next day; stir before using.

Tree Pear Purée. Drain 2 cans (about 1 lb. *each*) **pears in extra-light syrup;** reserve 1½ cups of the syrup and discard remainder. In a small pan, combine reserved syrup and 1 **star anise** or 1 teaspoon anise seeds. Bring syrup to a boil over high heat; then reduce heat, cover, and simmer very gently until flavors are blended (about 10 minutes). Pour syrup through a fine strainer set over a bowl; discard star anise or seeds. In a food processor or blender, whirl pears until smoothly puréed; then add syrup (if using a blender, add syrup while you are puréeing pears). Stir in ¼ cup **lemon juice** and 1 tablespoon **sugar**. If made ahead, cover and refrigerate until next day; stir before using.

Per serving: 187 calories (6% calories from fat), 2 g protein, 46 g carbohydrates, 2 g total fat (0 g saturated fat), 0 mg cholesterol, 19 mg sodium

Pictured on page 106

Sparkling Jewels Fruit Soup

Preparation time: About 10 minutes

Cooking time: About 5 minutes

This beautiful summertime dessert is easy to make: just float your choice of colorful fresh fruit in a clear, slightly sweet "broth" of white grape juice spiked with crystallized ginger.

> **Mixed Fruit (suggestions follow)**
> 2 **tablespoons lemon juice**
> 2 **cups white grape juice**
> 2 **tablespoons minced crystallized ginger**
> 3 **tablespoons orange-flavored liqueur**
> **Mint sprigs (optional)**

1. Prepare fruit of your choice. Place fruit in a large bowl and mix gently with lemon juice. (At this point, you may cover and refrigerate for up to 2 hours.)

2. In a small pan, bring grape juice and ginger to

a boil over high heat. Stir in liqueur; pour over fruit. Ladle soup into bowls; garnish with mint sprigs, if desired. Makes 4 to 6 servings.

Mixed Fruit. You need 2½ cups fruit *total*. We suggest using 1 large firm-ripe **kiwi fruit** (about 4 oz.), peeled and thinly sliced; ½ cup diced firm-ripe **nectarin**e or peeled peach; ⅓ cup **fresh or frozen unsweetened blueberries;** ⅓ cup thinly sliced hulled **strawberries;** and ⅓ cup very thinly sliced firm-ripe **plum.**

Per serving: 145 calories (2% calories from fat), 0.5 g protein, 33 g carbohydrates, 0.3 g total fat (0 g saturated fat), 0 mg cholesterol, 15 mg sodium

Double Caramel Flan

Preparation time: About 50 minutes, plus about 30 minutes to cool caramel

Cooking time: 1 to 1¼ hours

Chilling time: At least 4 hours

Our delicate, deep golden flan boasts a double dose of caramel. Like the traditional dessert, this version is sauced with caramel syrup—but it's also flavored with homemade caramel powder. If you like, you can even garnish the velvety custard with glistening chunks of crunchy caramelized sugar.

- ⅔ **cup Caramel Powder (recipe follows)**
- ⅓ **cup sugar**
- 2 **cups nonfat or lowfat milk**
- 6 **large eggs**
- 1 **teaspoon vanilla**
  Caramel chunks (optional; reserved from caramel used for Caramel Powder)

1. Prepare Caramel Powder and set aside.

2. Pour sugar into a wide nonstick frying pan. Place pan over medium heat; cook, shaking pan frequently to stir sugar, until sugar is melted and deep amber in color (3 to 5 minutes). Immediately pour syrup into an 8- to 9-inch, 1-quart or larger straight-sided baking dish or pan. Quickly rotate dish to coat bottom with syrup.

3. In a small pan, combine milk and Caramel Powder. Stir over medium-high heat until all caramel is melted (it will harden first)—about

7 minutes. In a bowl, whisk eggs and vanilla until blended. Whisk some of the hot milk mixture into eggs; then stir egg mixture back into pan. Remove from heat and pour into prepared baking dish. Set dish in a larger rimmed baking pan; then set pan on middle rack of a 350° oven.

4. Pour 1 inch of boiling water into larger pan. Bake until center of flan jiggles only slightly when dish is gently shaken (35 to 45 minutes). Lift dish with flan from water. Let cool; then cover and refrigerate for at least 4 hours or up to 2 days.

5. To serve, run a thin knife between flan and dish. Invert a rimmed platter over dish; holding platter and dish together, invert both. Carefully lift off dish; scrape any caramel left in dish over flan. Garnish flan with small chunks of caramel, if desired. Cut into wedges. Makes 8 servings.

Caramel Powder. Line a 10- by 15-inch rimmed baking pan with a single sheet of foil, folding foil up at edges.

Pour 2 cups **sugar** into a wide nonstick frying pan. Place pan over medium-high heat; cook, shaking pan frequently to stir sugar, until almost all sugar has liquefied (about 10 minutes). Reduce heat to medium; tilt pan to mix hot syrup with any remaining sugar until all sugar is melted and deep amber in color (3 to 5 more minutes).

Immediately pour hot caramel syrup into foil-lined pan. Using hot pads to protect your hands (mixture is very hot), tilt pan to spread syrup in a thin layer. Set aside until caramel is hard and completely cool (about 30 minutes).

When caramel is cool, lift foil from pan; peel foil from caramel. Break caramel into chunks; reserve a few pieces to garnish flan, if desired. Place remaining caramel in a blender or food processor (container must be completely dry) and whirl until pulverized; if you use a blender, you may need to make powder in several batches. Store powder airtight at room temperature for up to 1 month. Makes about 1¾ cups.

Per serving: 184 calories (19% calories from fat), 7 g protein, 31 g carbohydrates, 4 g total fat (1 g saturated fat), 161 mg cholesterol, 79 mg sodium

Pictured on page 127

Mexican Cocoa Cake

Preparation time: About 10 minutes

Baking time: 30 to 40 minutes

Delicious with a cup of Mexican Coffee (page 112), this rich-tasting cocoa cake features the cinnamon and almond flavors of traditional Mexican chocolate. For an extra treat, top each serving with lean, lightly spiced whipped "cream."

   Spiced Cream (optional; page 117)
 1 **cup sifted cake flour**
 ⅓ **cup unsweetened cocoa powder**
 1 **teaspoon *each* baking soda, baking powder, and ground cinnamon**
 6 **large egg whites**
 1⅓ **cups firmly packed brown sugar**
 1 **cup plain nonfat yogurt**
 2 **teaspoons vanilla**
 ¼ **teaspoon almond extract**
   Powdered sugar

1. Prepare Spiced Cream, if desired; refrigerate.

2. In a small bowl, mix flour, cocoa, baking soda, baking powder, and cinnamon. In a large bowl, beat egg whites, brown sugar, yogurt, vanilla, and almond extract until well blended. Stir in flour mixture and beat just until evenly moistened.

3. Pour batter into an 8-inch-square nonstick (or greased regular) baking pan. Bake in a 350° oven until center of cake springs back when lightly pressed (30 to 40 minutes). Let cake cool in pan on a rack for 15 minutes; then invert it onto a serving plate. Serve warm or cool. If made ahead, wrap cooled cake airtight and store in a cool place until next day (freeze for longer storage).

4. Just before serving, sift powdered sugar over cake. To serve, cut cake into wedges or rectangles. If desired, sift more powdered sugar over each serving; then top with Spiced Cream, if desired. Makes 8 servings.

Per serving: 227 calories (3% calories from fat), 6 g protein, 51 g carbohydrates, 1 g total fat (0.4 g saturated fat), 1 mg cholesterol, 293 mg sodium

Pictured on facing page

Drunken Cake

Preparation time: About 10 minutes

Baking time: About 20 minutes

This single-layer cake is flecked with orange peel and soaked with a cinnamon-scented orange-rum syrup. It's a perfect warm-weather dessert—and just as good in any other season, especially after a spicy meal. If you like, garnish the cake with orange segments just before serving.

   Spirited Syrup (recipe follows)
 2 **large eggs**
 ½ **cup sugar**
 ¾ **cup all-purpose flour**
 1½ **teaspoons baking powder**
 2 **tablespoons grated orange peel**
 ¼ **cup butter or margarine, melted**
   Orange segments (optional)
   Mint sprigs

1. Prepare Spirited Syrup; set aside.

2. In a food processor (or in a large bowl), whirl (or beat) eggs and sugar until thick and lemon-colored. Add flour, baking powder, orange peel, and butter; whirl (or beat) until well blended. Spread batter in a greased, floured 9-inch cake pan with a removable rim. Bake in a 375° oven until cake just begins to pull away from sides of pan and center springs back when lightly pressed (about 20 minutes).

3. Set warm cake in pan on a rack; set rack over a plate to catch any drips. Pierce cake all over with a fork. Slowly pour Spirited Syrup over cake; let cool. Just before serving, remove pan rim. Garnish cake with orange segments, if desired, and mint sprigs. Makes 8 servings.

Spirited Syrup. In a small pan, mix ¾ cup **sugar,** 1 teaspoon grated **orange peel,** ½ cup **orange juice,** ½ teaspoon grated **lemon peel,** 2 tablespoons **lemon juice,** and ⅛ teaspoon **ground cinnamon.** Bring to a boil over medium-high heat. Boil, stirring, just until sugar is dissolved. Remove from heat and let cool; then stir in 2 to 3 tablespoons **light or dark rum** and 1 teaspoon **vanilla.**

Per serving: 259 calories (27% calories from fat), 3 g protein, 43 g carbohydrates, 8 g total fat (4 g saturated fat), 69 mg cholesterol, 167 mg sodium

*Glistening with a citrusy rum syrup and scented with fresh orange,
our Drunken Cake (recipe on facing page) is a wonderful conclusion to a
spicy dinner. Cut the moist layer into wedges to serve with strong,
hot coffee or aromatic tea.*

BEVERAGES

Some are chilly, some steaming hot—but all the Mexican-style beverages on these pages are delightfully lean. To sip before or during meals, choose tangy iced tea, zesty lemonade, or cold fruit punch. Sample margaritas in two forms—one spirited, the other nonalcoholic. And to start or finish any day perfectly, linger over a mug of Mexican coffee or cocoa.

Pictured on page 10
HIBISCUS ICED TEA

Jamaica flowers—the dried, deep red calyxes of hibiscus blossoms—give this drink its vivid scarlet hue.

- 2 **quarts water**
- 24 **bags herbal tea containing hibiscus flowers**
- ½ **cup sugar**
- ¼ **cup lime juice**
  Crushed ice
  Lime slices or wedges

1. In a 3- to 4-quart pan, bring water to a boil over high heat. Add tea bags, sugar, and lime juice.

2. Remove from heat, cover, and let cool. Discard tea bags. Pour tea into ice-filled glasses; top with lime slices. Makes 6 to 8 servings.

Per serving: 66 calories (0.3% calories from fat), 0.1 g protein, 20 g carbohydrates, 0 g total fat (0 g saturated fat), 0 mg cholesterol, 30 mg sodium

PRICKLY PEAR PUNCH

This spirited punch showcases rosy red prickly pears. If you can't find them (they're available in Mexican markets and some well-stocked supermarkets from August through December), substitute cranberry juice cocktail for the prickly pear purée.

Red Prickly Pear Purée (page 108); or 4 cups chilled cranberry juice cocktail
- 2 **bottles (about 750 ml. *each*) chilled brut champagne or sparkling wine**
- 1 **to 2 quarts chilled sparkling water**
  Crushed ice (optional)

1. Prepare Red Prickly Pear Purée; cover and refrigerate until cold (about 2 hours) or until next day. Pour into a pitcher.

2. Present purée with chilled champagne and sparkling water. Mix by the glass, filling each glass one-third full of purée. Then slowly add enough champagne, water, and ice (if desired) to fill glass to rim. Makes about 12 servings.

Per serving: 152 calories (8% calories from fat), 1 g protein, 17 g carbohydrates, 0.7 g total fat (0 g saturated fat), 0 mg cholesterol, 15 mg sodium

Pictured on page 71
CHILE-MINT LEMONADE

Sweet, spicy, and tart flavors combine in this unusual lemonade.

- 6 **cups water**
- ¾ **cup sugar**
- 1½ **cups coarsely chopped fresh mint**

- 4 **to 8 small dried hot red chiles**
- 1 **cup lemon juice**
  Mint sprigs
  Crushed ice

1. In a 3- to 4-quart pan, combine 2 cups of the water, sugar, chopped mint, and chiles. Bring to a boil over high heat; then boil, stirring occasionally, until reduced to 1 cup (12 to 14 minutes).

2. Remove from heat, let cool, and pour through a fine strainer into a pitcher. Press residue to extract liquid. Discard mint; rinse chiles and add to pitcher along with lemon juice and remaining 4 cups water. Cover and refrigerate until cold (at least 1 hour) or for up to 1 week.

3. Serve lemonade in pitcher or in a tall decorative bottle; add a few mint sprigs to serving container. Pour into ice-filled glasses; garnish each serving with more mint sprigs. Makes 4 to 6 servings.

Per serving: 132 calories (3% calories from fat), 0.5 g protein, 34 g carbohydrates, 0.4 g total fat (0 g saturated fat), 0 mg cholesterol, 11 mg sodium

Pictured on page 114
MEXICAN COFFEE

Though traditionally brewed in an earthenware pot or *olla*, Mexican coffee—fragrant with cinnamon and sweetened with brown sugar—can also be made successfully in a drip-style coffee maker.

- 5 **to 7 cinnamon sticks (*each about 3 inches long*)**
- ½ **cup ground regular or decaffeinated coffee**

1 cone piloncillo (about 3 oz.), chopped; or ¼ cup firmly packed brown sugar

4 cups water

1. Break one cinnamon stick in half. Place coffee in filter container of a drip-style pot; then scatter broken cinnamon stick and piloncillo over coffee.

2. Brew coffee with 4 cups water. Pour into 4 to 6 cups; garnish each serving with a cinnamon stick. Makes 4 to 6 servings.

Per serving: 46 calories (0.2% calories from fat), 0.2 g protein, 12 g carbohydrates, 0 g total fat (0 g saturated fat), 0 mg cholesterol, 7 mg sodium

MEXICAN HOT COCOA

Capture the essence of Mexico's famous, foamy chocolate drink in this lean hot cocoa. To keep the drink frothy and well mixed, pour and serve it as soon as you've whirled it in the blender.

½ cup *each* sugar, unsweetened cocoa powder, and water

½ teaspoon ground cinnamon

4 cups nonfat milk

½ teaspoon vanilla

¼ teaspoon almond extract

1. In a 1½- to 2-quart pan, combine sugar, cocoa, water, and cinnamon. Bring to a boil over medium-high heat, stirring until sugar and cocoa are completely dissolved. Stir in milk, then stir over medium heat just until steaming; do not boil.

2. Remove pan from heat and stir in vanilla and almond extract. Pour half the hot milk mixture into a blender or food processor and whirl until very frothy; pour into mugs and serve at once. Repeat with remaining milk mixture. Makes 4 to 6 servings.

Per serving: 171 calories (10% calories from fat), 8 g protein, 34 g carbohydrates, 2 g total fat (1 g saturated fat), 4 mg cholesterol, 103 mg sodium

Pictured on page 31

SPIRITED MARGARITAS

Mexico's best-known cocktail is doubtless the margarita, a refreshingly tart drink based on tequila and lime. Always serve your margaritas in well-chilled glasses, rimmed with salt for tingling flavor. (Or, if you prefer, coat the glass rims in sugar.)

Salt-rimmed glasses (directions follow)

¾ cup *each* lime juice and tequila

½ cup orange-flavored liqueur

3 cups crushed ice

4 lime wedges or slices

1. Prepare 4 salt-rimmed glasses.

2. In a cocktail shaker or blender, shake or whirl lime juice, tequila, liqueur, and ice until very cold.

3. Pour drinks into salt-rimmed glasses (if drink is shaken, you can pour it through a strainer and discard ice). Garnish each serving with a lime wedge. Makes 4 servings.

Salt-rimmed glasses. Rub rims of 1-cup-size glasses with a **lime or lemon wedge** or moist shell of a squeezed lime or lemon. Have **coarse salt** or sugar on a flat plate. Dip glass rim into salt or sugar. Refrigerate until serving time.

Per serving: 197 calories (2% calories from fat), 0.1 g protein, 12 g carbohydrates, 0.1 g total fat (0 g saturated fat), 0 mg cholesterol, 8 mg sodium

NONALCOHOLIC MARGARITAS

This ice-cold, slushy cocktail has all the flavor of the famous margarita, but none of the "punch."

Salt-rimmed glasses (above)

1 can (about 12 oz.) frozen limeade concentrate

About 2 cups crushed ice

1 can (12 oz.) nonalcoholic beer

6 lime wedges or slices

1. Prepare 6 salt-rimmed glasses.

2. In a blender or food processor, whirl limeade concentrate and ice until ice is very finely crushed. Blend in beer (if your blender isn't big enough to hold all the beer, add only part of it).

3. Pour drinks into salt-rimmed glasses; divide any remaining beer equally among glasses. Garnish each serving with a lime wedge and serve at once. Makes 6 servings.

Per serving: 148 calories (0.5% calories from fat), 0.4 g protein, 39 g carbohydrates, 0.1 g total fat (0 g saturated fat), 0 mg cholesterol, 1 mg sodium

Pictured on page 87

PINEAPPLE RUM PUNCH

Though designed for the cocktail hour, this rum punch is perfect at mealtimes, too.

1 can (about 12 oz.) frozen pineapple juice concentrate, thawed but still cold

¾ cup *each* nonfat milk and canned unsweetened coconut milk

About ¾ cup light rum, or to taste

⅓ cup lime juice

3 cups chilled sparkling water

Crushed ice

Pineapple spears (optional)

1. In a blender, whirl pineapple juice concentrate, nonfat milk, coconut milk, rum, and lime juice until smooth. Pour into a 3-quart pitcher and stir in sparkling water. Add ice to make punch as cool as you like.

2. To serve, pour punch into glasses. Garnish each serving with a pineapple spear, if desired. Makes 12 servings.

Per serving: 131 calories (27% calories from fat), 1 g protein, 18 g carbohydrates, 3 g total fat (3 g saturated fat), 0.3 mg cholesterol, 12 mg sodium

Served warm from the oven, Cinnamon Bread Pudding with Pumpkin Custard (recipe on facing page) is one of the best ways we know to round out a cold-weather feast. Mexican Coffee (recipe on page 112) is the perfect complement for this homey dessert.

Cinnamon Bread Pudding with Pumpkin Custard

Preparation time: About 15 minutes

Baking time: About 1 hour and 35 minutes

Warm up a winter meal with this hearty dessert. The moist pudding is easy to assemble; while it bakes, stir up a smooth pumpkin custard to enhance each serving.

- 2 **large eggs**
- 2 **large egg whites**
- ⅓ **cup sugar**
- 1½ **cups** *each* **lowfat buttermilk and nonfat milk**
- 2 **teaspoons vanilla**
- 1 **teaspoon ground cinnamon**
- 8 **slices raisin bread or whole wheat bread, cut into 1-inch pieces**
- ½ **cup raisins or dried currants (optional)**
  Pumpkin Custard (recipe follows)
  Ground nutmeg (optional)

1. In a large bowl, beat eggs, egg whites, sugar, buttermilk, milk, vanilla, and cinnamon until blended. Add bread; then stir in raisins, if desired. Let stand for 5 minutes to soften bread. Transfer mixture to an 8- or 9-inch-square nonstick (or greased regular) baking pan.

2. Set pan of pudding in a larger baking pan; then set pans on middle rack of a 325° oven. Pour boiling water into larger pan up to level of pudding. Bake until top of pudding is golden brown and center no longer jiggles when pan is gently shaken (about 1 hour and 35 minutes).

3. When pudding is almost done, prepare Pumpkin Custard. Spoon warm custard into 8 dessert bowls or plates and spoon pudding on top; ladle more custard over pudding, if desired. Sprinkle with nutmeg, if desired. Makes 8 servings.

Pumpkin Custard. In a 1½- to 2-quart pan, mix ½ cup **sugar** and 2 tablespoons **cornstarch.** Stir in 2 cups **nonfat milk,** 1 can (about 1 lb.) **pumpkin,** and ¼ teaspoon **ground nutmeg.** Bring to a boil over medium-high heat, stirring. Remove from heat and whisk in 2 large **egg whites.** Return to heat and cook, stirring, just until mixture is bubbly and beginning to thicken. Remove from heat and stir in 1 teaspoon **vanilla.** If desired, firmly rub custard through a fine strainer set over a bowl. Serve hot or warm.

Per serving: 273 calories (12% calories from fat), 11 g protein, 49 g carbohydrates, 4 g total fat (0.9 g saturated fat), 58 mg cholesterol, 251 mg sodium

Raisin Rice Pudding

Preparation time: About 5 minutes

Cooking time: 50 to 65 minutes

Creamy rice pudding flavored with cinnamon and vanilla is a favorite Mexican dessert. Serve it warm or chilled; it's delicious either way.

- 3½ **cups nonfat milk**
- ½ **cup short- or medium-grain rice**
- ¼ **teaspoon salt**
- 3 **large eggs**
- ¼ **cup sugar**
- 2 **teaspoons vanilla**
  About ¼ teaspoon ground cinnamon
- ¼ **cup golden or dark raisins**
- 1 **tablespoon honey**

1. In a 1½- to 2-quart pan (preferably nonstick), combine 3 cups of the milk, rice, and salt. Bring just to a very gentle boil over medium heat, stirring. Reduce heat to low, cover, and simmer, stirring occasionally, until mixture is reduced to 2¾ cups (45 minutes to 1 hour).

2. In a bowl, beat eggs, sugar, remaining ½ cup milk, vanilla, and ¼ teaspoon of the cinnamon until blended. Stir in raisins.

3. Stir egg mixture into rice mixture. Bring just to a boil, then reduce heat and simmer, uncovered, until thickened (about 5 minutes). Stir in honey. Serve warm or chilled. Sprinkle with additional cinnamon just before serving. Makes 6 servings.

Per serving: 213 calories (12% calories from fat), 9 g protein, 37 g carbohydrates, 3 g total fat (1 g saturated fat), 109 mg cholesterol, 197 mg sodium

Cherry Chimichangas

Preparation time: About 10 minutes

Baking time: 8 to 10 minutes

Cherries and cherry preserves fill these crisp treats, delicious with cocoa or coffee.

- 2 teaspoons berry-flavored liqueur
- 1 or 2 teaspoons cornstarch
- ¼ cup cherry or strawberry preserves
- 1 teaspoon grated lemon peel
- 2 cups pitted, chopped fresh cherries; or 2 cups frozen pitted dark sweet cherries, thawed, chopped, and drained well
- 6 flour tortillas (7- to 9-inch diameter)
  About ⅓ cup nonfat milk
  Powdered sugar

1. In a bowl, stir together liqueur and cornstarch until smooth (use 1 teaspoon cornstarch if using fresh cherries; use 2 teaspoons cornstarch mixed with 2 teaspoons water if using thawed frozen cherries). Stir in preserves, lemon peel, and cherries.

2. To assemble each chimichanga, brush both sides of a tortilla liberally with milk; let stand briefly to soften tortilla. Place a sixth of the filling on tortilla. Lap ends of tortilla over filling; then fold sides to center to make a packet. Place chimichanga, seam side down, on a lightly oiled 12- by 15-inch baking sheet; brush with milk. Repeat to make 5 more chimichangas.

3. Bake in a 500° oven, brushing with milk twice, until golden brown (8 to 10 minutes). Let chimichangas cool slightly, then dust with sugar and serve warm. Makes 6 chimichangas.

Per chimichanga: 207 calories (13% calories from fat), 4 g protein, 41 g carbohydrates, 3 g total fat (0.5 g saturated fat), 0.3 mg cholesterol, 176 mg sodium

Dessert Nachos

Preparation time: 15 to 20 minutes

Cooking time: About 10 minutes

For a quick and festive dessert, spoon fruit salsa and a honey-sweetened cream cheese sauce onto crisp flour tortilla chips sprinkled with sugar and cinnamon.

> **Cinnamon Nacho Chips (recipe follows)**
> **Fruit Salsa (recipe follows)**
- 1 large package (about 8 oz.) Neufchâtel or cream cheese
- ½ cup orange juice
- 3 tablespoons honey

1. Prepare Cinnamon Nacho Chips and Fruit Salsa.

2. In a small pan, combine Neufchâtel cheese, orange juice, and honey. Whisk over low heat until sauce is smooth (about 3 minutes).

3. Mound chips on a platter. Offer sauce and salsa to spoon onto chips. Makes 10 to 12 servings.

Cinnamon Nacho Chips. In a shallow bowl, mix ⅓ cup **sugar** and 1 teaspoon **ground cinnamon**; set aside. Dip 10 **flour tortillas** (7- to 9-inch diameter), one at a time, in water; let drain briefly. Stack tortillas; then cut stack into 6 to 8 wedges. Dip one side of each wedge in sugar mixture. Arrange wedges in a single layer, sugared side up, on lightly oiled 12- by 15-inch baking sheets; do not overlap wedges. Bake in a 500° oven until crisp and golden (4 to 5 minutes). If made ahead, let cool; then store airtight at room temperature for up to 3 days.

Fruit Salsa. Hull 2 cups **strawberries**; dice into a bowl. Add 2 large **kiwi fruit** (about 8 oz. *total*), peeled and diced, and about 1 cup diced **orange segments**. Cover and refrigerate until ready to serve or for up to 4 hours.

Per serving: 229 calories (14% calories from fat), 8 g protein, 42 g carbohydrates, 4 g total fat (0.5 g saturated fat), 4 mg cholesterol, 330 mg sodium

Lemon & Tequila Sherbet

Preparation time: About 15 minutes

Cooking time: About 5 minutes

Freezing time: At least 4 hours

A special meal deserves a dramatic finale like this one: scoops of tart lemon sherbet served in pools of icy-cold tequila. When you're planning your cooking schedule, be sure to allow ample time for freezing the sherbet.

1 envelope (about 2 teaspoons) unflavored gelatin

3 tablespoons cold water

1 cup sugar

2 cups water

2 teaspoons grated lemon or lime peel

⅔ cup lemon or lime juice

About ⅓ cup white tequila, chilled in freezer until ice-cold

Thin lemon or lime slices

1. In a small bowl, sprinkle gelatin over cold water; let stand until softened (about 5 minutes). In a small pan, combine sugar and the 2 cups water. Bring to a boil over high heat; then reduce heat, cover, and simmer for 5 minutes. Add gelatin and stir just until dissolved; stir in lemon peel and lemon juice. Let cool, then pour into 2 divided ice cube trays and freeze until firm (at least 4 hours) or for up to 3 days; cover mixture once it's solid.

2. Loosen cubes from trays; scoop cubes out of trays with a spoon, if needed. (If cubes are very hard, let stand at room temperature until slightly softened—about 2 minutes—before removing.) Place cubes in a food processor or a bowl; whirl or beat with an electric mixer until smooth.

3. Serve sherbet soft; or cover airtight and refreeze until firm (about 1 hour) or for up to 1 week. To serve, scoop sherbet into stemmed dessert glasses or small bowls and drizzle with tequila to taste. Garnish with lemon slices. Makes 6 to 8 servings.

Per serving: 145 calories (0.4% calories from fat), 0.9 g protein, 30 g carbohydrates, 0.1 g total fat (0 g saturated fat), 0 mg cholesterol, 6 mg sodium

Pictured on page 122

Oranges with Rum Syrup & Spiced Cream

Preparation time: About 15 minutes

Cooking time: About 20 minutes

Freezing & chilling time: 45 minutes to 1 hour

A sweet rum syrup infused with cloves is served over orange slices for a refreshing dessert. Garnish each serving with a dollop of whipped "cream."

Spiced Cream (recipe follows)

½ cup sugar

1½ cups water

2 teaspoons whole cloves

2 tablespoons light rum

4 large oranges (about 3 lbs. *total*)

1. Prepare Spiced Cream; refrigerate.

2. In a small pan, combine sugar, water, and cloves. Bring to a boil over high heat; then boil until reduced to ¾ cup (about 20 minutes). Remove from heat, stir in rum, and let cool. (At this point, you may cover and refrigerate for up to 5 days.)

3. With a sharp knife, cut peel and all white membrane from oranges. Slice fruit into 6 dessert bowls, dividing equally. Add rum syrup and Spiced Cream to taste. Makes 6 servings.

Spiced Cream. Pour ¼ cup **nonfat milk** into small bowl of an electric mixer. Cover bowl; then freeze mixer beaters and bowl of milk until milk is slushy (30 to 45 minutes). In a small pan, sprinkle ½ teaspoon **unflavored gelatin** over ¼ cup **cold water;** let stand until gelatin is softened (about 3 minutes). Then stir mixture over low heat just until gelatin is dissolved. Remove from heat.

To slushy milk, add gelatin, ⅔ cup **instant nonfat dry milk**, 2 tablespoons **sugar**, 1 teaspoon **vanilla**, and ½ teaspoon **ground cinnamon**. Beat on high speed until mixture holds soft peaks (5 to 10 minutes). Cover and refrigerate for at least 15 minutes or for up to 2 days. If needed, whisk or beat again before serving until cream holds soft peaks. Serve cold. Makes about 2 cups.

Per serving of oranges: 153 calories (2% calories from fat), 1 g protein, 36 g carbohydrates, 0.4 g total fat (0.1 g saturated fat), 0 mg cholesterol, 0.6 mg sodium

Per tablespoon of Spiced Cream: 10 calories (1% calories from fat), 0.6 g protein, 2 g carbohydrates, 0 g total fat (0 g saturated fat), 0.3 mg cholesterol, 9 mg sodium

A P P E N D I X

Though Mexican food is fairly familiar to most home cooks, you'll probably encounter at least a few ingredients that will spark questions: "What is this? What does it look like? Where can I buy it?" For help with these queries, refer to the following pages.

Because chiles are so important in Mexican cooking, we begin with a guide to fresh and dried chiles, including illustrations and descriptions of a number of types. We then move on to a discussion of other ingredients, from achiote and blue corn to tomatillos and tortillas. Using the information here, you'll soon become acquainted with the ingredients that are new to you; you'll also learn a bit more about the Mexican foods you already know and use.

Chile de arbol

California

Chile negro
(dried pasilla)

Cascabel

Ancho

Mulato

Tepin

Dried
New Mexico

California

Pequin

Chipotle

Mulato

Red

Habanero

Guajillo

Santa Fe Grande

Poblano

Serrano

Thai

Anaheim

Green jalapeño

Red (ripe) jalapeño

*The fresh and dried chiles shown here are just a sampling of the hundreds
of mild to fiery varieties grown around the world.*

119

Chiles

Chiles are the heart, soul, and fire of Mexican cooking. They're among the world's most popular flavorings, and in Mexico alone, hundreds of varieties are grown. Our recipes call for only a few of the most common types, but if you do find the other kinds listed (or if you grow them at home), this guide will help you use them.

In North America, many people think of chiles as exclusively hot seasonings and assume that anything containing them will be tongue-searing. But Mexican cooks use chiles to impart mild and subtle flavors, too. Once you've learned something about the various chile types and how to prepare them, you'll be able to produce authentic-tasting dishes with just the heat level you like.

Chiles get their heat from a substance called capsaicin, found in the interior veins near the seed heart. Contrary to common belief, the heat isn't in the seeds themselves; the seeds are often hot because they're close to the veins. By removing both veins and seeds, you can tone down the chile's heat.

Though smaller varieties of chiles are generally hotter than larger ones, heat levels may differ even within a variety, depending on the climate and soil. And of course, the human palate varies too: a chile that tastes fiery to one person may seem mild to another.

Fresh chiles. When selecting fresh chiles, choose those that are firm, smooth, and glossy, with no splits or signs of withering. To keep the chiles fresh at home, enclose them in a plastic bag, then refrigerate for up to 1 week.

When you handle fresh chiles, protect your hands with rubber gloves and avoid touching your face or eyes. If any skin does come in contact with chile oil, thoroughly wash the affected area with soap and water.

To make stuffed chiles (*chiles rellenos*) and various other dishes, you'll need to start by roasting and peeling the chiles. There are three ways to do this. *First,* you can place the chiles on a baking sheet and broil them 4 to 6 inches below the heat, turning often, until the skin is charred and blistered all over (5 to 8 minutes). *Second,* if you have a gas range, try holding the chiles with tongs and turning them, one at a time, over the flame until they're blackened and blistered (1 to 1½ minutes). *Finally,* if you're working with a large number of chiles, arrange them slightly apart on baking sheets and bake, uncovered, in a 450° oven, turn-ing several times, until the skins are brown and blistered (20 to 30 minutes).

Once the chiles have been roasted, cover them airtight with foil while they're still hot. Let them stand until they're cool enough to handle; then carefully peel off the skins and remove and discard the stems, veins, and seeds. Use the chiles at once, or cover and refrigerate them for up to 3 days (freeze for longer storage).

Dried chiles of several varieties, usually sold in cellophane bags or in bulk, are easily as important in Mexican cuisine as the fresh peppers. In Mexican grocery stores, you'll find them near the spices; in well-stocked supermarkets, look in the Mexican products section or alongside the fresh produce. The dried chiles you buy should look pliable, not cracked or overdry. If you see powder in the bag, the chiles may be old.

Ground chile (true "chili powder") is sold in markets carrying Mexican products, but you can make it at home if you like. Begin by roasting whole dried chiles on a baking sheet in a 350° oven until very dry and crisp (5 to 10 minutes), turning once or twice. When the chiles are cool enough to handle, break them into pieces, discarding the stems, seeds, and veins. Grind the pieces to a fine powder in a blender or coffee grinder; store the powder in a cool, dark place (be sure to label the container, noting which type of chile you used).

NOTE: In this book, we spell the word "chile" with a final *e* when referring to the fresh or dried fruit. "Chili" is the spelling used for commercial chili powder—a mixture of ground dried red chiles, cumin, oregano, and other seasonings—and for the famous stewlike dish from the Southwest.

Chile Varieties

What do you call *that* chile? The question seems straightforward, but the answer isn't easy. Chile nomenclature is far from standardized: several different names may be used for one kind of chile, and a single type may have different names in its fresh and dried forms. We hope the following descriptions help clear up a little of the confusion.

Anaheim (also called California, New Mexico, or Rio Grande green chile). Probably the most popular and widely available fresh chile in the United States, the Anaheim has a mild to medium-hot flavor. Much of the crop is processed for sale as canned green chiles. Fresh Anaheims are bright green, turning to red as they ripen; they vary somewhat in size and shape, but most kinds are 6 to 7 inches long and pointed at the tip. When dried, they're usually called dried California or New Mexico chiles (like the fresh chiles, the dried ones may vary in shape and size).

Ancho (also called poblano and mulato; often confused with pasilla chiles). This large, triangular, mahogany-colored chile is the dried form of the fresh poblano chile. It's most commonly used for making mole sauces.

Bahamian. See Habanero.

California (also called Anaheim). Dried Anaheim chiles are generally marketed as "dried California chiles." Like dried New Mexico chiles (see below), California chiles are typically roasted, then soaked in hot liquid and puréed before use in cooking.

Cascabel. Round and pungent, this Mexican chile is usually sold dried in Mexican grocery stores. When the chile is shaken, its seeds rattle—hence the name *cascabel* ("jingle bells" in Spanish).

Cayenne. These thin, fiery-hot, 2- to 3-inch-long chiles are typically marketed dried, either whole or ground into powder. Commercial "cayenne pepper" often contains a mixture of several hot chiles, and is therefore labeled "ground red pepper."

Chile de arbol. Small and quite hot, chiles de arbol are similar to cayenne chiles (above). The name—literally, "tree chile"—refers to the plant's resemblance to a small tree.

Chipotle. *Chipotle* isn't really a chile variety; it's the name given to dried, smoked red jalapeños. You can find whole dried chipotles in Mexican markets and (more recently) in well-stocked supermarkets, but they're more typically sold canned—in *adobo* or *adobado* sauce (a tomato-based sauce) or *en escabeche* (in a pickling mixture).

Fresno (sometimes called hot chile; may be confused with jalapeño and Santa Fe Grande chiles). Named for the place they were first grown— Fresno, California—these small chiles are bright green, turning to red as they ripen. Fresnos look much like jalapeños and make a good substitute for them, though they're slightly milder in flavor.

Guajillo (also called mirasol). A dried brownish-orange chile frequently sold in Mexican markets, the guajillo has a distinctive fruity-hot flavor. Fresh guajillos are commonly called mirasol chiles.

Guero (sometimes confused with jalapeño or Santa Fe Grande chiles). *Guero* means "blond" in Spanish—and the guero chile is pale yellow to yellow-green, ripening to dark red. Hot to fiery in flavor, these 1- to 5-inch-long chiles can substitute for jalapeño, serrano, or Santa Fe Grande chiles.

Habanero (also called Scot bonnet or Bahamian chile). Thought to have originated in the Caribbean, the lantern-shaped habanero is now raised primarily in the Yucatán. It's sold pickled and, more recently, both fresh and dried. Habaneros can be blisteringly hot (the hottest types are more potent than any other chile), so use them with caution.

Jalapeño. First grown in Jalapa in the state of Veracruz, the jalapeño is a popular hot chile both north and south of the border. Most markets sell jalapeños fresh, canned, and pickled; in some stores, you may also find them dried and smoked (in this form, they're called chipotle chiles; see above). Fresh jalapeños are 2½ to 3½ inches long, turning from bright green to red with ripening. They're a fine substitute for most other hot chiles. Pickled jalapeños add a lively accent to salads, sandwiches, and other dishes.

Japanese. See Red.

Japones. See Red.

Mirasol. The word translates as "look to the sun"—an apt description of the way this chile's fruit tends to stand erect on the plant. The mirasol group comprises a number of different chiles; you'll often see the name used for fresh guajillos (see above).

Mulato (also called poblano or ancho; often confused with pasilla chiles). Mild to medium-hot in flavor, the mulato is a type of poblano chile. It's large and fleshy, turning from dark green to brown as it ripens; when fresh, it's excellent for chiles rellenos and other dishes made with mild to fairly spicy chiles. Dried mulatos have a dark chocolate-brown color; in Mexico, they're often made into a paste and sold for use in mole sauces.

New Mexico (sometimes called California or Anaheim chile). Like Anaheims, these large chiles turn from green to scarlet as they mature. They resemble Anaheims in flavor, too, though they are somewhat spicier. In Mexican markets, you may see the ripe chiles strung into ropes or *ristras* and hung to dry.

Light, lovely Oranges with Rum Syrup & Spiced Cream (recipe on page 117) are worthy of your prettiest dessert glasses. Serve with thin slices of moist Raisin Batter Bread (recipe on page 105).

You'll find green New Mexico chiles fresh, canned, and frozen. The fresh chiles are excellent in salsas and for chiles rellenos or any other mildly spicy chile dish—but it's the dried version, harvested at the red stage, that's more typically called for in recipes. Like dried California chiles, the dried New Mexico type is usually roasted, soaked, puréed, and added to stews and sauces. Dried New Mexico chiles may also be pulverized and sold as ground New Mexico chile.

Pasilla (often confused with poblano, ancho, or mulato chiles; labeled *chile negro*—"black chile"— when dried). The name of this mild to medium-hot chile is surrounded with confusion. And in fact, the name itself may be part of the problem: the word *pasilla* means "little raisin," and by extension, it has come to be used for many wrinkled-looking dried chiles. Nonetheless, there is a true pasilla chile, quite different from poblanos, anchos, and other chiles you may see labeled "pasilla." Genuine pasillas are thin, 5- to 7-inch-long chiles, dark green when fresh, black when dried. Most are sold in dried form; they're a good substitute for ancho and mulato chiles.

Pequin (also called chile piquin). These tiny, oval, fiery-hot chiles are primarily used for commercial liquid hot pepper seasoning. The green fruits are generally pickled, while the red (ripe) ones are dried; Mexican markets carry both forms. Dried pequins may be substituted for cayenne chiles, tepins, and chiles de arbol.

Poblano (also called ancho and mulato; often confused with pasilla chiles). Triangular in shape and mild to medium-hot in flavor, poblano chiles measure 3 to 5 inches long and 2 to 3 inches wide at the stem end. The fruit starts out a very deep, almost blackish green, but color at maturity varies. Some types ripen to red; these are called ancho chiles when dried. Another kind, the mulato chile, is brown when ripe.

Like Anaheims and New Mexico chiles, poblanos are well suited for chiles rellenos and other recipes calling for large, mild to moderately spicy chiles.

Red (also called Japanese or japones). This small dried hot chile resembles the chile de arbol and the cayenne chile.

Sandia. The tapering, 5- to 7-inch-long Sandia can be used interchangeably in cooking with fresh Anaheim and New Mexico chiles. It's typically

sold ripe—when it's bright red. In the Southwest, Sandias are sometimes used to make jelly.

Santa Fe Grande. These chiles resemble Fresnos in heat level and size and are interchangeable with them in cooking. The color differs, though. Fresnos turn from green to red as they ripen, while Santa Fe Grandes start out yellow, then ripen to red.

Scot bonnet. See Habanero.

Serrano. These slender chiles resemble small jalapeños, but their flavor is slightly hotter. In color, they're a bright light to dark green, ripening to red, brown, orange, or yellow. Serranos are usually sold fresh or pickled; the fresh chiles are used in salsas and sauces, while the pickled ones make a lively condiment. Serranos can substitute for jalapeño, Fresno, and Santa Fe Grande chiles.

Tepin (also called chiltepin). Tiny (from about ¼ inch to ½ inch in diameter), round, and very hot, tepin chiles are sometimes found dried in Mexican markets. They can be used in place of cayenne chiles, pequins, or chiles de arbol.

Thai. The name "Thai chile" is sometimes given to the tiny, hot red and green chiles used in Southeast Asian cooking. Fresh Thai chiles are becoming increasingly available in well-stocked supermarkets.

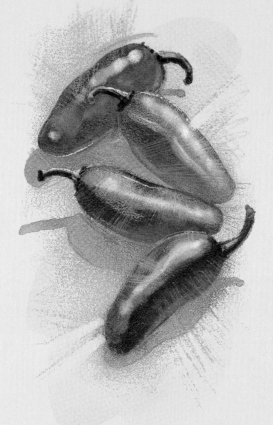

Other Mexican Ingredients

Achiote. Brick-red achiote seeds come from the annatto, a tropical tree native to Mexico. Before use, the seeds must be soaked overnight in water, then puréed to make a paste. Like paprika, achiote adds a red hue and a subtle, earthy flavor to the dishes in which it's used. Look for achiote seeds, achiote condiment, and achiote paste alongside the other seasonings in Mexican markets. For a recipe using achiote (and instructions for making an achiote substitute), see Tamale Pie (page 22).

Asadero. *See* Cheese.

Atole. *See* Blue corn.

Blue corn. A staple in Mexico, earthy-flavored blue corn is usually dried and ground into meal or flour for making tortillas and other baked goods with a distinctive gray-blue to deep blue color. The meal is sold in two grinds: *harina para tortillas* (coarse) and *harina para atole* (fine). Before purchasing blue cornmeal, check your recipe to see if it specifies one grind or the other.

In recent years, blue cornmeal has become increasingly available in well-stocked natural-foods and specialty grocery stores. If you can't find it, you can order it by mail from the following two sources: Casados Farms, Box 852, San Juan Pueblo, New Mexico 87566, (505) 852-2433; or G. B. Ratto & Co., International Grocers, 821 Washington Street, Oakland, CA 94607, (510) 832-6503.

For blue cornmeal recipes, see page 104.

Chayote. This tropical summer squash has been a cultivated crop for centuries, at least since the time of the Aztecs. It's a pale green, pear-shaped vegetable with deeply furrowed skin; the flavor is mild, similar to that of zucchini. To prepare chayote, simply rinse the fruit well; then slice it right through the seed, which is edible. Steam or boil chayote as you would summer squash. It's good when stuffed with meat or other fillings, as in Chayote with Turkey (page 70).

Cheese. Mexican cooks commonly use several cheeses. A number of these are sold in the United States; of the available types, many are produced in California. Look for them in Mexican markets and well-stocked supermarkets.

Queso fresco ("fresh cheese"; also called *ranchero*) is the most widely distributed variety.

It's lumpy and mild-flavored, similar to farmers cheese or mild feta. Enjoy it on its own, sliced or coarsely shredded; or crumble it on tacos, enchiladas, chiles rellenos, eggs, hot beans, or salads.

Asadero is a buttery-tasting string cheese—sometimes stretched and rolled into balls, sometimes shaped into logs and sold in tortilla-size slices. It's similar to mozzarella, though tangier.

Oaxaca is a mild, slightly dry string cheese; like asadero, it's reminiscent of mozzarella, though it's not as creamy.

Cotija (also called *queso seco*, "dry cheese") is a dry, crumbly cheese, similar to Parmesan but with a milder taste.

Panela, a simple cheese of drained clotted curds, tastes much like dry cottage cheese; use it as you would queso fresco or mild feta.

Chorizo. These spicy fresh pork sausage links are sold in butcher shops and most supermarkets. Chorizo can also be made at home; on page 56, you'll find a lightened-up turkey version (it's made in bulk, not shaped into links). Serve chorizo plain or use it in sauces and fillings (see Tinga, page 24, and Turkey Chorizo Enchiladas, page 20).

Cilantro. Also called coriander or Chinese parsley, this pungent herb adds a distinctive flavor to numerous Mexican dishes. It's sold fresh all year round in most supermarkets.

Cornhusks. Indispensable for making tamales, cornhusks are usually sold dried in Mexican grocery stores and markets offering a good selection of Mexican products. The husks must be soaked before use.

Cotija (queso seco). *See* Cheese.

Epazote (sometimes called wormseed or goosefoot). This medicinal-tasting herb is used in the cuisine of the Yucatán peninsula. Fresh epazote is hard to find in American markets, but it can easily be grown from seed. Look for the dried herb in Mexican markets.

Hominy (also called pozole or posole). Sold dried, frozen, and canned, hominy is nothing more than large dried white or yellow corn kernels that have been soaked in a lime solution to remove their hulls. The partially cooked frozen product has the best flavor, but it's typically found only in some Mexican markets. The dried form is somewhat more available in Mexican markets, while canned hominy is readily available in almost all supermarkets.

Jamaica. The small, dried, deep red calyxes of the hibiscus flower are used in Mexico to make scarlet-hued drinks such as Hibiscus Iced Tea (page 112). Dried jamaica is available in Mexican markets and well-stocked supermarkets. Stored airtight in a cool, dry place, it will keep for up to 6 months.

Jicama. A popular Mexican root vegetable, jicama looks like a giant brown turnip. Its thick, rough skin conceals crisp, white, slightly sweet flesh that's reminiscent of water chestnuts in both texture and flavor. Typically served as an appetizer or snack with lime and salt or other dips, it can also be used as an ingredient in recipes.

Masa & masa harina. Masa is the corn dough used to make tortillas and tamales; it can be purchased premixed in some Mexican markets as well as at some tortilla factories. Masa harina, marketed by the Quaker Oats Company (the name is a registered trademark), is a dehydrated corn flour that can easily be made into masa.

Nopales (cactus leaves or paddles). The flat, prickly, light green leaves of the prickly pear cactus are available fresh in Mexican markets and, occasionally, in well-stocked supermarkets. You're more likely to find them canned, though, either pickled or packed in water. In this form, they're referred to as *nopalitos* (nopales that have been diced or cut into strips).

Oaxaca. *See* Cheese.

Panela. *See* Cheese.

Pepitas. Pepitas—edible pumpkin seeds—are a common ingredient in Mexican cooking. *Pipian*, a popular sauce for fish, wild game, chicken, and pork, is based on pepitas; the seeds are simply ground together with chiles, spices, and herbs. Pepitas are sold raw or toasted, salted or unsalted, and with or without hulls. They're available in natural-foods stores, Mexican markets, and well-stocked supermarkets.

Piloncillo. Piloncillo is unrefined sugar shaped into hard, brown cones. Sold in Mexican markets and well-stocked supermarkets, it's used to sweeten Mexican Coffee (page 112) and some desserts. Wrapped airtight, the cones will keep indefinitely.

Pine nuts (also called piñons or pignolias). Small, oval, cream-colored pine nuts come from the piñon pines native to, among other regions, Mexico and parts of the Southwestern United States. Because the nuts are actually inside the pine cones, removing them is a laborious process—one reason why pine nuts tend to be so expensive. Still, there's no substitute for these distinctive nuts in authentic Mexican dishes. Pine nuts are sold shelled (and sometimes in the shell), either in bulk or alongside the other packaged nuts in supermarkets and Mexican markets. They're highly perishable, so purchase only small quantities.

Pozole. *See* Hominy.

Prickly pears (also called cactus pears or tunas). Prickly pears are the fruit of a native Mexican cactus. The skin is bright red; the juicy, delicately sweet flesh is a deep magenta or red-purple. The fruit must be peeled before use (wear rubber gloves to protect your hands from the spines).

You'll find prickly pears in Mexican markets and some well-stocked supermarkets from August through December. For recipes featuring prickly pears, see pages 108 and 112.

Queso fresco (ranchero). *See* Cheese.

Queso seco (cotija). *See* Cheese.

Ranchero (queso fresco). *See* Cheese.

Tomatillos. Tomatillos resemble small green tomatoes enclosed in papery husks. Tart and slightly fruity in flavor, they're the basic ingredient in numerous sauces and salsas. Many well-stocked supermarkets carry both fresh and canned tomatillos; you'll find the fresh fruit in the produce section, the canned product with the Mexican foods. To prepare fresh tomatillos for use, remove the papery husks and stems; then rinse each fruit well to remove its sticky coating.

Tortillas. In Mexico, these thin flatbreads are served at every meal. The traditional corn tortilla is shaped by hand from masa (see above), but the machine-shaped corn and flour tortillas sold in most markets are excellent, too. Besides the usual corn and white wheat-flour types, some manufacturers offer tortillas of other kinds—blue corn, whole wheat, and sprouted wheat, for example. For more information on tortillas, see page 25.

Index